SECOND CHANCE

HOW TO MAKE <u>AND KEEP</u> BIG MONEY FROM
THE COMING GOLD AND SILVER SHOCK-WAVE

DAVID H. SMITH AND DAVID MORGAN

ISBN: 978-1-4834-6035-2 (sc)
ISBN: 978-1-4834-6036-9 (hc)
ISBN: 978-1-4834-6034-5 (e)

Library of Congress Control Number: 2016917376

Lulu Publishing Services rev. date: 10/24/2016

"I skate to where the puck is going to be, not where it has been."

"The Great One" Canadian NHL legend, Wayne Gretzky

CONTENTS

ACKNOWLEDGEMENTS

It would be impossible to list all of the people who have been of help to us - by dint of their thinking and accomplishments - in our path on this writing journey. Looking back we are amazed at just how many capable and honorable individuals populate the resource sector space. From a sector sometimes maligned by the public for its presumed lack of transparency and opaque operating procedures, these individuals, all of whom we are proud to say we know either professionally or personally, are without a doubt some of the very best. Suffice to say that it has been their collective wisdom and willingness to share that has added immeasurably to our own experiences and enabled us to write a book of this nature. For this we thank you individually and collectively.

Our book was not just written as a contemporary piece, or for the immediate future, but hopefully to help people - especially the Baby Boomers and the Millennials - to move successfully into the years leading up to and through the Great Gate of historical sociopolitical transformation that the authors discuss in their book *The Fourth Turning*, and about which we devote a chapter in our book.

We have each raised two Millennials, and we're happy to say that we have maintained strong, adult relationships with them now that they are moving to their own drummers in life. They have been and remain a great gift to us. Now, in this small but hopefully relevant way, we want to acknowledge our responsibility to help out. This is because we wish to be of service in facilitating their acquisition of the financial means of moving forward, as we all face the daunting, yet transformative changes - hopefully for the better - of an unknown future. We acknowledge the debt we owe them, as well as to our own Boomer generation - and we are committed to doing our very best in their behalf.

We would like to offer special thanks to barcharts.com, stockcharts.com, Palisade Global, Nick Laird at goldchartsurus.com, the World Gold Council, U.S. Global Investors, Neil Howe (The Fourth Turning), and Doug Casey (Casey Research) and Rambus, for the courtesy of having their charts and passages included in this book. The serious student of this subject matter will find what these sources offer - both in the public domain or by subscription - to be of great value. We would also like to extend our thanks to Steven A. Smith for providing a number of the fine drawings for our text. And finally our appreciation for Dr. Keith Barron's unexpected and very helpful decision to offer his suggestions before the final cut.

PREFACE

As last year drew to a close, it began to dawn on me (David Smith) that my investment activity in the financial markets, the writing I was doing for various Internet venues, my ongoing studies of history, politics and the martial arts, and personal efforts to remain in optimum health, had a certain unity of purpose.

On the surface these strands might have looked to be separate, but they were actually weaving themselves into a "life-rope" of sorts, guiding me on toward a denouement in time and space. Furthermore, I was (am) not alone on this trip, for being on the leading edge of the so-called Boomer generation, I share a place on life's journey that by the nature of my physical age, places me in proximity with millions of similar souls.

By definition, the Boomer cohort is moving through its life cycle as a social tsunami phenomenon. Since my brother, Bill (around 1998) gave me a copy of *The Fourth Turning: An American Prophecy - What the Cycles of History Tell Us About America's Next Rendezvous with Destiny*, I have come to see how powerful is its premise, how comprehensive its research, how informative it can be for those who seek a "window" and eventually a "door" into the future - for our country, ourselves, and our children.

David Morgan and I are both "Boomers". We have each raised two Millennials, as we witnessed the changes through which our nation has been moving over the last few decades. Society has made great strides, but more and more we seem to be moving in the wrong direction for all but the relative few, who've come to be called "the Protected Class", the "1%", or some other less savory name. To be clear, the "wealthy" per se should not be spoken of disparagingly, because the end result for honest people who accumulate significant wealth through ethical means, is that their efforts benefit both themselves and the nation. In fact the opportunity to raise oneself up economically has been a cornerstone expectation throughout much of American history.

But a certain number of bankers, financiers, government employees, and politicians nowadays seem to exist - not to help others, but simply to line their own pockets, and increase their power over others - doing so in a way that makes it look like they will never stop and say "This is enough." When they break the law - often times on an epic scale - they seldom go to jail, or pay a fine commensurate with their misdeeds. If forced to account publicly, they usually blame someone or something else, seldom accepting any guilt. Even in the rare instance when they do take responsibility, the only consequence seems to be a comparatively modest fine. However, throughout history, a display of this kind of attitude has never been helpful in maintaining social cohesion or encouraging peaceful relations with the rest of the population. One of these days, something *has* to give... and it will.

Around 2000, this writer walked into a coin shop to engage in a conversation with the owner as to whether the price of silver would ever rise from the dead, let alone approach the $50 mark it had briefly struck two decades earlier. We didn't reach any conclusions, but I did notice that something had been left on the counter by another customer. It was a photocopy of a lengthy article (from a series) written by James Puplava, titled "The Perfect Financial Storm, Part 5: Rogue Wave". It addressed what the author felt was an evolving financial tempest heading toward U.S. economic shores. His definition of the rogue wave was visually evocative. It set in motion a powerful desire to watch that wave build, get on it, and ride its transformative powers - which would at once be destructive, yet also creative in a new paradigm sense - to a potentially life-altering financial bonanza. Even now, Puplava's description conveys a vivid picture as strongly as it did that day in the coin shop. He wrote,

> "There will come a day unlike any other day, an event unlike any other event and a crisis unlike any other crisis. It will emerge out of nowhere at a time no one expects. It will be an event that no one anticipates- a crisis that the experts didn't foresee. It will be an exogenous event -- a rogue wave."

Nowadays, quite a few analysts and investors actually do foresee great storms and stress heading our way - Doug Casey calls it a hurricane. Most of the population, from the average Joe, to the scions of finance and politics still seem to be rather clueless. We're quite certain this state of affairs is going to change markedly... and soon.

David Morgan and I talked about writing a book dealing with how to successfully trade the precious metals' bull run for well over a decade - indeed clear back in 2001, when silver was just beginning to stir from its 20 year bearish slumber. We wanted to discuss not only how to buy, hold and trade gold, silver and the mining stocks, but also <u>how to keep</u> as much of those earnings as possible. Looking at our separate experiences in the 1980 market, we knew what a great feeling it was to make a lot of money on paper, but we also saw how fast it evaporated once the primary trend changed from up to down. The 2000 dot com mania demonstrated the same kinds of behaviors - people getting caught up in a massive bull run, overstaying their welcome, riding the bear trend down, and giving back much if not all they had earned beforehand.

We felt there must be a better way...

We knew that most people - even those who get in on a big trend early - do not take much money out of the market. It's like they get to feeling so comfortable with being right that they can't stand the idea of getting out when the market has proven that indeed, they were! They have to stay around until all or most of their money disappears.

We've had two big legs up in silver, first to $22 in 2008; then to just under $50 in 2011, with gold exceeding $1,900. We've suffered through a 5 year cyclical bear market that cleared out most of the erstwhile bulls. Now it looks like we're going to see the third and biggest upside move of all. On the way, gold will play tag team, an absolutely essential role in causing silver to make its own mirror image moon shot. As for the mining stocks - well many of those are going to have an outer space price launch that may create a book of records all its own.

At this point we don't know exactly how high they will go or how long it will take. But it almost doesn't matter. If you can take a big chunk out of the middle, and still hang in there with a portion of your investible funds - handling them in a special way which we'll describe later on in great detail - the results could end up being <u>beyond</u> spectacular.

We're going to be walking our talk - committing our own money - riding that wave for all it's worth. Would you care to join us?

FOREWORD

Recently I have been involved in a project concerning the world's earliest coinage, dating from circa 650-700 BC, made from electrum, an alloy of gold and silver by the Lydians. Man's love affair with gold and silver though, extends back even further to the Egyptian Pharaohs, the Babylonians, the Scythians, the Sumerians and other cultures. Its origins are lost in history, but it has been revered, venerated, prized, defended, and even considered holy for millennia. Gold and silver are part of our cultural DNA, and though various transitory governments contrive and conspire to ignore it, do away with it, or even threaten death to possessors, we seem to revert to a cultural mean each time after these governments fade away, where once again precious metals regain their lustre.

It's __not__ different this time!

What *is* different though, is that the current cloud-seeding by governments and the deluge of fiat money drenching us will result in unprecedented precious metal investment opportunities never before experienced in all of modern history. Today we see a parade of ad hoc "fixes" being trotted out by governments for fiscal dilemmas without any coordinated or long term plan. The only objective is to provide some quasi-stability while said government is still in office. Whether or not the US Federal Reserve or the ECB like it, a good proportion of the world is fed up with monetary experiments and have already gone to precious metals as a safe haven and safeguard against the profligacy of world governments.

The One (gold and silver) Ring (Courtesy Steven A. Smith)

Janet Yellen can't undo 5000 years of history. Even if the Western-trained economists of today are buying into John Maynard Keynes' pronouncement of gold as a "barbarous relic", many other cultures didn't get the memo. My own belief is that the emergence of the middle classes in India and China – those cultures who "backwardly" see gold and silver as stores of value, will dynamite the Comex and other paper markets. A time will come, and I don't believe it is far off, when the "We Buy Your Gold" shops in the West have drained almost everything and sent it East. Ditto for World Gold Production, scheduled to fall off a cliff in 2017 due to lack of investment in mine-building and exploration over the last 5 years. These are not possibilities; they will indeed happen! It is "baked in the cake".

It's "baked in the cake."

As a footnote or a parting thought, please consider this: Janet Yellen and her confederates will not go down without a fight. We have already seen words like "prudence", "frugality", "thrift", and phrases like "fiscal responsibility" vanish from the American lexicon of government-speak. Expect words like "opportunists", "carpetbaggers", "robber barons", "unscrupulous", "unethical", "unpatriotic" and "unfair" to be applied to gold and silver investors with increasing vigour by populist politicians. We will be demonized by a financially inept and morally bankrupt group of persons more concerned with self-aggrandisement than governing.

Expect piled on capital gains taxes, wealth taxes, windfall profits taxes, and any number of surtaxes to descend on you. Nobody will give a damn that you invested your hard-earned after-tax money wisely, they will first tax your profit, then they will tax your principle. When you make profits don't keep it all in 401K's and RRSP's. Get some of it "off the grid" where future governments can't grab it. I'm not advocating not paying your taxes today, but just don't expect the present rules to always remain the same. Remember France's 75% Super Tax that President François Hollande brought in and then repealed? Oh ya, it's not just Third World countries that do this.

Stay the course with precious metals! Ignore the background noise, and as my late Father always advised, "Put it away safe, and then sit back and read the comics."

Dr. Keith M. Barron, August 26, 2016.

INTRODUCTION

Shock-Wave

There is a tide in the affairs of men, Which taken at the flood, leads on to fortune. Omitted, all the voyage of their life is bound in shallows and in miseries. On such a sea are we now afloat. And we must take the current when it serves, or lose our ventures. -**William Shakespeare**

Tsunami is a Japanese term meaning "harbor wave." Less correctly known as a "tidal wave", the tsunami results from a large-scale realignment which may be caused by an earthquake on the ocean floor far at sea, a volcanic eruption, or a meteorite's impact. A wave, or a series of them (actually a vertical water <u>column</u>) is unleashed, moving rapidly away from its point of origin.

Because of low amplitude, this water column moving past and under a small boat at sea might hardly be noticed. But the wave itself, with only a small energy loss, would be traveling along at several hundred miles per hour - bending as it heads toward land with the water's depth varying near the crest.

Keep this analogy in mind as you read this book. You're going to learn how to "paddle out into the water" so that the "quickening financial tsunami" passes beneath you with little effect.

Especially destructive tsunamis tend to have long wavelengths (the distance between waves), known as "wave periods". Approaching shore they bunch up or "shoal", increasing in speed and height. Upon making landfall, a surging mass of water is driven deeply inland.

Shortly before a tsunami's secondary impact, seawater along the coastline may withdraw, giving the appearance of an extremely low tide. During such an interim, people lower their vigilance and begin acting as if this unusual situation is both normal and safe. They may traipse out onto exposed areas and even lose themselves beachcombing.

The "interim period" we've witnessed in the global arena has been taking place since 2008, when near-disastrous effects of the first financial tsunami struck our shores and began to recede. It will end when the next shock-wave, more devastating than the first hits, and paralyzes the global financial system. It's headed our way right now.

Within a short time, the water mass - now traveling at the speed of a fast cyclist - hits the shallows, unleashing an enormous wave carrying everything before it. Near population centers, massive damage and casualties are the rule. Once its initial force is spent, the tidal flow moves away from the coast and an eerie calm ensues.

The worst MUST be over, right? But no - this could be just the beginning! A succession of "follow on" waves - <u>with swells often several times larger than the initial surge</u>, and mixed with wreckage sucked out by the first deluge, form return waves and slam against the shoreline, causing even greater damage. During these ensuing strikes, which can space from a few minutes, to over an hour apart, the REAL DESTRUCTION takes place.

The 2004 tsunami in the Indian Ocean hit landfall hundreds of miles from its point of origin, with rollers up to 50 feet high and took over 250,000 lives. The monster tsunami striking Japan in March, 2011, killed more than 20,000 people and released an environmental contagion, conceptually like the "financial toxins" unleashed in 2008 that affects us to the present day.

This sequence of events and the way people react to it are repetitive and predictable. Look at video footage of the infamous December 2004 tsunami which struck communities along the coastlines of Indonesia, Sri Lanka, India, and Thailand. A wall of water generated by a gigantic earthquake off the coast of Sumatra battered the coastline, carrying everything before it. Video recordings at far-flung locations provide evidence of mistaken actions - or inaction - that cost many people their lives.

After the initial surge during the 2004 tsunami, people walked out into the mess, leaving elevated positions of safety as the water receded.

They continued to drive along cluttered coastal roads, and climbed down from their perch on tall buildings. A short time later another bigger surge returned with a vengeance, claiming as victims, many who had escaped the initial flood.

An especially poignant scene remains forever etched in our memory. Someone with a camcorder from atop an embankment filmed the scenery across a broad, sandy beach. He/she panned across the valley, taking in the expanse of sand, as a series of normal waves lazily moved in from seaward. A solitary man can be seen walking toward the shore with his back to the water. Several hundred yards behind him, an enormous crest builds.

Continuing to walk at a measured pace, he has absolutely no inkling of the looming menace speeding behind him toward shore. The towering wave crests and breaks onto the beach, driving in tidal-bore fashion, as he continues walking - still without a clue! A torrent of foam-crested water, brown with mud, sand and debris, silently and swiftly envelopes the hapless individual and carries him away without a trace!

The Japanese have a saying, "It's an ill wind (or wave) that blows no good." If that's the case - and we believe it is - You should be able to survive - even thrive during the "follow - on" economic, political and social change-waves which have been building ever since the economic tsunami struck the global system with devastating force in 2008 - and are now headed directly our way. After the deluge, you can be counted among the relative few who will have the resources to help build a new and more rational financial and socio-political structure that benefits the greatest number of its citizens.

In 2008, the first wave of the Global Economic Tsunami Struck

In late 2008, the global financial system literally came within hours of imploding as banks at all levels stopped lending, even to their best customers. Major financial institutions teetered on the verge of bankruptcy - or like Lehman Brothers and Bear Stearns collapsed. In just a few hours, half a billion dollars in money market funds surged out of customers' accounts. Of that period, the *(UK) Guardian* described it accurately, saying:

> It was the year the neo-liberal economic orthodoxy
> that ran the world for 30 years suffered a heart attack

of epic proportions. Not since 1929 has the financial community witnessed 12 months like it. Lehman Brothers went bankrupt. Merrill Lynch, AIG, Freddie Mac, Fannie Mae, HBOS, Royal Bank of Scotland, Bradford & Bingley, Fortis, Hypo and Alliance & Leicester all came within a whisker of doing so and had to be rescued.

Western leaders, who for years boasted about the self-evident benefits of light-touch regulation, had to sink trillions of dollars to prevent the world banking system from collapsing. The ramifications of the Banking Collapse of 2008 will be felt for years if not decades to come...

The movie *The Big Short* was a huge box office success. The scriptwriters got a lot of things right. They noted how close the short sellers came to running out of time and money before their ideas about an implosion of the financial system came to fruition. If several large brokerages and banking houses had gone down like dominoes for the count, these speculators, while being correct on their premise, might never have collected, with the result that both they and their backers would have been swept off the map.

But the most important concept was not even mentioned. It was that were it not for the easy money policies of the Federal Reserve, then the real estate, stock market and derivatives binge the shorts were betting against could never have scaled the lofty price peaks they managed to reach. Yet now we have one of the prime architects of that disaster, Alan Greenspan, known as the "Maestro", telling us that the problems are still with us, and that we "should own gold"!

Most of us have some awareness of the re-inflating asset bubbles in commercial and residential real estate, the bond market, sub-prime car loans and student debt. While this is going on, Japan's central bank has become the primary customer for <u>negative</u> interest-bearing bonds. Trillions of dollars in the Eurozone have the same "yield". Amazingly, this circumstance is a first in recorded history. Europe's largest bank is on the ropes; Italy's banking sector stands at the edge of a cliff. The U.S., with 20 trillion dollars in debt, talks (seriously) of "helicopter money". We could name a dozen more systemic issues - and so could you!

The 2009 - 17 "Wave Period" is coming to an end.

We've seen that a given tsunami may not consist of just one wave, but several - with successive breakers becoming larger and more dangerous than the ones which proceeded it.

The idea of the Big Wave coming out of nowhere that catches people by surprise, disorients, and sweeps them (and their material goods) into oblivion is a fitting analogy for what faces us as we look at the current global financial landscape. An understanding of how human nature operates when faced with a "sea change" is critical if we are to prepare for, take advantage of and successfully "ride" such a monster.

In reality, there is almost always a warning - sometimes several - that a big financial dislocation is in the air. But human nature seems to mandate that most people either down-play or totally ignore the signals until it's too late to do anything.

As this is being written, "change-waves" are beginning their run. A dislocating systemic transformation is in the air, fated to stand on its head what we assume will happen or think we know. The great global commodity boom that began with the 21st Century carried prices of many natural resources to multiples of where they stood just a decade before - and then in a full-sector collapse of epic proportions, fell into an abyss.

Some of these adjustments were beneficial - at least for the winners. The former Soviet Union, after collapsing in 1980, paid off its foreign debt and now boasts one of the largest gold holdings of any country in the world. It suffered through a series of wrenching currency devaluations - largely shielded by the rising value of gold holdings, and the ability to earn critical foreign exchange through the sale of oil and natural gas. So far, it's still on its feet.

China's tumultuous century saw it disintegrate from Dynastic to Warlord rule, and nearly buckle under invasion by the Japanese, followed by a revolutionary metamorphosis leading to 5 decades of Communism and 70 million deaths. Now it's evolving into a quasi-capitalist - authoritarian state. In less than twenty years, its economic expansion has been so rapid it's GDP has overtaken that of the U.S. In spite of charges that bureaucrats have been falsifying growth figures, that "ghost cities" remain unoccupied and bad debts put on by zombie industries multiply, Beijing moves forward.

In the process, they've managed for a decade to remain the world's largest gold producer, and are now the largest gold importer as well. By almost any measure, quite a change for a nation once derisively known as "The Sick Man of Asia".

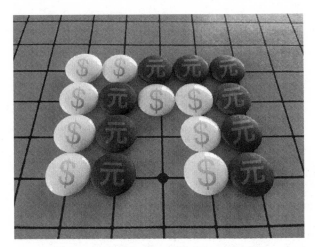

Chinese Go Stones- Yuan vs. $USD

The New Silk Road

For fifteen centuries, commerce between China and Europe was conducted along a network of roadways called the Silk Road. The coming of modern air, land and shipping routes superseded these old transport arteries. But now China, in concert with Russia and other Far East players, intends to revive these connections, in what may become the largest construction project in history.

Known by the Chinese as "One Belt, One Road", or the Belt and Road Initiative, the plan, described as an *"economic partnership map with multiple rings interconnected with one another"* envisions an economic land belt and a maritime road linking Beijing through Europe to the Mediterranean. This modern equivalent of the old Silk Road would weave together the economies of over half the world's population via transit corridors of highways, high-speed rail, fiber-optic cables, pipelines, and air and seaport hubs.

As if these plans were not unsettling enough to Western central banks, China is instituting an international payments system (CIPS) with its own credit card, lending and banking (AIIB) entities - a direct challenge to SWIFT, the U.S. Interbank clearing system for international money and security transfers.

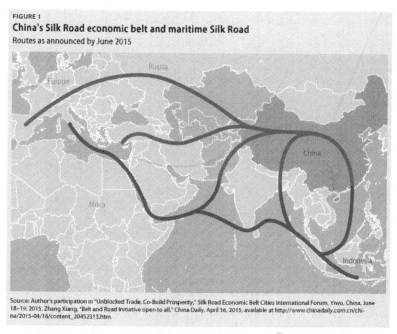

FIGURE 1
China's Silk Road economic belt and maritime Silk Road
Routes as announced by June 2015

Source: Author's participation in "Unblocked Trade, Co-Build Prosperity," Silk Road Economic Belt Cities International Forum, Yiwu, China, June 18–19, 2015. Zhang Xiang, "Belt and Road Initiative open to all," China Daily, April 16, 2015, available at http://www.chinadaily.com.cn/china/2015-04/16/content_20452313.htm.

China's Belt and Road project (Courtesy chinadaily.com)

To say the New Silk Road's completion would be an economic game-changer of the first magnitude would be an understatement. It has the potential to strategically redraw the global imperatives of the last few centuries, wherein for many countries, control of the seas and its shipping lanes were literally matters of life and death. The implications for gold and silver will be multi-dimensional. The commodities sector could benefit once again as construction of the Belt and Road continues in future years.

Political tension will increase as China challenges the supremacy of the West. This will cause a concomitant increase in demand for gold and silver for use in trade, savings and as a possible underpinning for currencies and layers of derivatives. Socio-economic and political disruptions, both positive and negative, are destined to have a profound impact on the upward trajectory of the metals and mining stocks for years to come.

As a companion approach to understanding the seismic changes underway in "the Far East" we highly recommend Marin Katusa's book, *The Colder War: How the Global Energy Trade Slipped from America's Grasp.* In it he presents a highly perceptive look at the drivers which motivate Vladimir Putin - and anyone who might follow him, as Russia moves forward in its campaign for energy dominance on the Euro-Asian land mass. An old Russian aphorism "Despotism tempered by assassination - that is our Magna Carta", plus a careful reading of *The Colder War,* will provide you with a well-grounded perspective about the direction of Russia's past, present... and future.

Ripples in the Global Pond

The free market represents the sum total of all participants - individuals, businesses, banks and nation-states - operating in their perceived self-interest over time. When certain aspects of the system become oppressive, develop systemic contradictions that might lead to lock-up or implosion, or no longer make economic sense to stakeholders, evolutionary change eventually gets underway. In the process, some of these changes have the potential to bring about a sea change in "the way things have always been done." The dynamic behind the New Silk Road is just one of several.

Another one to watch is the concept behind "Ripple." Ripple is one of several financial blockchain technologies being tested and developed, in league with several mega-banks, to serve the perceived need for simplifying cross-border payments and financial transactions. The developers and involved banks hope to launch this protocol commercially within 2 years. Business will be conducted directly bank to bank, rather than through currently-controlled U.S. systems, which are subject to political pressure, and are more costly, complicated, less nuanced and less flexible than will be the case with the new blockchain operating systems. Depending upon the success of these efforts, and of the financial entities underpinning development of the New Silk Road, the result could be a devolution of the U.S. global financial system as it has operated since Bretton Woods. Stay tuned and stay nimble...

Ride the coming financial paradigm shift

Jim Rickards is one of the most astute - and listened to - observers in the resource sector space today. His broad connections within the "deep state" as well as the investment community, enable him to view both sides of the coin from the edge, or third side, as Robert Kiyosaki would say, that few others can equal. We highly recommend (in addition to reading our book!) that you take time to carefully study Jim's highly-readable work, *The New Case for Gold.*

We, like Rickards feel that the price and supply windows for acquiring gold and silver are in the process of closing. The metaphor he uses certainly strikes a note with us, to wit:

> The time to act is now… A new crisis is a mathematical certainty, but I can take it further… what you don't hear is this will be exponentially larger than any financial panic in the past… The next time, the Fed is going to be in trouble. They are already insolvent on a mark-to-market basis. Each bailout gets much bigger than the one before. The Fed has a 10-foot seawall, and they are going to get hit with a 50-foot tsunami.

A financial paradigm shift is underway, with the trend now firmly entrenched by the grinding together of demographic and supply-demand tectonic plates. What's beginning to take place in one specific investment sector as these mega-events play out, and how it will affect you is the subject of this book. You may have been financially crushed in the 2008 near-collapse of the global economy. You may be struggling just to maintain a reasonable standard of living, let alone improve it. What's coming next will be much worse. You need to prepare now.

As this destructive seismic apparition heads for landfall, you have an opportunity to ride it with confidence while others stand rooted to the spot. You can take steps to protect your assets the way people have effectively done for thousands of years. Only now you'll be armed with the technology of the Internet, newly-developed trading platforms, and effective analytical tools to limit risk and magnify profit potential. You can emerge from the destruction of the Old Financial Order with the resources to help build a new one.

Richard Russell: Newsletter Writer Extraordinaire

In support of our thesis, we would like to add a quote from perhaps the longest-published, most prolific financial newsletter writer in the business, Richard Russell. After publishing his Dow Theory Letters since 1958, he passed away in late 2015, at age 91. His words should help guide us - and you - as we accept the challenges and potential that the financial markets are presenting to us. He wrote:

> I have never seen a bull market of this size end without a highly-speculative third phase explosion. What we see on the chart over the last few years is a huge accumulation pattern in the shape of a head and shoulders bottom... Somewhere ahead I expect to see a worldwide panic-scramble for gold as it dawns on the world population that they have been hoodwinked by the central banks' creation of so called paper wealth... In their heart of hearts, men know this. Which is why, in experiment after experiment with fiat money, gold has always turned out to be "the last man standing."

By adding our perspective to what you already know how to do for yourself, and heeding the call for action, you're going to have a Second Chance. By learning *How to Make **and Keep** Big Money from the Coming Gold and Silver Shock-Wave.*

We are in the intermediate to late stages of a massive secular up-move in the price of gold - and especially silver. It is important to understand what has taken place in the fundamentals of these markets since the last bull run ended in 1980, and get a clear picture of the changing environment that investors face this time around.

Armed with this knowledge, it is possible during the next few years, for informed investors to make trading decisions with the potential of achieving stellar returns. But it gets even better…Silver's price appreciation potential is so outstanding that even average investors can entertain the idea of making enough money to effect a change of financial destiny - for themselves - and their loved ones. Get ready to read and appreciate our next chapter - "The Case for Silver."

CHAPTER 1

The Case For Silver

Silver has a very high potential of again multiplying wealth fabulously in the coming years. Mean reversions are one of the most powerful forces in all the markets. The more extreme the deviation from the mean, the bigger the subsequent reversion in the opposite direction to restore normalcy to the relationship. Silver's upside is vast given its recent extreme lows. - Adam Hamilton

An entire book could be written on the case for silver, and in fact a few have been, basically making the case that silver is probably "the best investment" one could make - bar none. In most of these writings there are a few flaws. First and foremost is the idea the silver has been in a continual deficit since the day it was first discovered - though this is a slight exaggeration on my part (David Morgan). It is a point of fact that a previous book—*The Silver Manifesto,* was written in 2015 to be a complete overview of silver from any aspect one would consider.

If there is one crucial factor that investors in the silver market need to know, it is simply this: Silver is not presently in a shortage! In fact the lowest above ground silver supply year was 2006. Since then, until this current writing, above-ground silver supply has grown by 1.5 billion ounces - and we are talking about investment grade silver! As of 2016, the amount available, both in coin and bar form is roughly two billion ounces.

There is another important point that few in the industry actually stress, which is the fact that while the overall supply of INVESTMENT

1

silver is much less than INVESTMENT gold, the overall amount of silver above ground is roughly five times greater! The amount mined is roughly ten times greater, but approximately half has been lost, mostly having been discarded in landfills, because the amount of silver per unit in things like older cell phones, computers, RFID chips, etc. was too small to be economically recycled.

Understanding the Silver "deficit"

Before leaving the topic of the silver deficit, it needs to be explained in greater detail. It is very likely you have read and will continue to read that the consumption of silver is greater than (mining) production. This in fact is absolutely true, but without more information many silver investors are left with the impression that it is only a matter of time before the world runs out of silver, and then its price will supposedly exceed that of gold.

However, it is the rest of the story that is of crucial importance! There is a great deal of silver recycled annually, which at the current time, is roughly between 150 and 200 million ounces. People need to understand that there are *two* silver supply chains - the mining industry and the recycling industry. When using the TOTAL supply to determine what is really going on in the silver market, they are astonished at the simple fact that, in most cases, supply meets demand, and that in addition, the above ground silver supply has been growing during the past decade.

Can Silver be in surplus and in deficit at the same time?

Another area which causes a great deal of confusion is the use of the word "deficit". There are two major silver studies produced each year, which are several multiples of the cost of *The Morgan Report*. In one you will see that silver is in a deficit, and in the other that it is in a surplus. Can they both be correct? Yes, depending upon how the accounting is performed. If you consider silver's investment demand to be part of total demand on an annual basis, then you can say the market is in deficit. However, if you look at the same investor supply, and see that the number of above ground ounces is growing year over year, it is consider to be in surplus.

So, rather than decide for you, let us state again, that the above ground supply of silver is growing. However, investors are buying and holding a great deal relative to annual production, so from that standpoint, silver indeed is in a very tight supply situation. In other words, silver is in very strong hands, and the number of "strong hands" is growing month over month.

100 troy oz Silver bar; 1 troy oz Canadian Silver Maple Leaf

Some investors may think that this truth about the silver market makes it a less desirable investment than the "silver shortage" story that is so pervasive on the Internet. However, knowing as many facts as possible about an investment, helps an investor to make the most informed decisions. Because the supply of silver above ground is growing, does not mean it is a poor investment. This is because the reason for investing in silver is nearly identical to that of investing in gold... and for all practical purposes the gold supply has been growing for centuries!

So why do people invest in gold - and silver? Because it is the most trusted and sought after monetary asset known to the global population for thousands of years! However, the actual truth of the matter is that silver, not gold, has been the real monetary asset for several millennia, and it has in reality, transacted far more business than gold!

This gives silver a unique advantage over all other precious metals. Gold has a monetary value known by investors, banks, and governments. Silver has a monetary value *and* an industrial value; in fact slightly more than half the silver mined every year is used by industry. If we add on the investment demand, we find that silver can quickly move up in price when investors worldwide decide to increase their holdings of the kind of money they can trust under any conditions.

There are a couple of factors which make an extremely compelling investment case for silver. The first is that silver is a very small market; the second is its volatility - how fast it can move in price. What we witnessed in the last bull market is that silver moved from $6 to $50 in only five months' time. As I have often stated, ninety percent of the move comes in the last ten percent of the time. This was certainly true of the previous bull market, but of course it is not a guarantee for the current bull market.

However, we do know that markets in general accelerate during the last few months of their bull run due to investors behaving with a herd mentality. In the case of a silver run, it could be because investors are concerned about the safety of their pensions, due to weakness in the global financial system, because of an unstable stock market, the fear (or an actual occurrence of) of bank holidays, or a bank "bail-in", which could deprive people of much of their savings.

Sooner or later, every fiat currency introduced has - and will - fail

If you are reading this book, we presume you are aware that through all of recorded history, every fiat currency in the world has sooner or later failed. Therefore, some margin of safety is required for those investors who truly understand the present-day world, which means that we think a ten percent allocation to the precious metals sector is sufficient for almost everyone.

At some point, the gold market will catch fire and the run to gold will begin in earnest. Once this occurs, the Midas metal will be in the mainstream financial press and many new potential investors will become aware of gold's move upward in price. The old adage that "there's no fever, like gold fever" will be appropriate, because at some point, enough of the world's investing community will have lost faith in the system at large, that they will begin to drive funds into the gold (and silver) markets across the board. Funds will flow heavily into physical gold, futures, ETF's, mining shares, and almost anything related in even the slightest way to precious metals. This occurrence is quite rare, and only takes place in monetary history when there is a near total breakdown of confidence in a country's monetary system.

Once this process begins, even the Working Group on Financial Markets (known caustically as "the plunge protection team"), or any other authority will have little chance of stopping the massive outflow of funds seeking safety. This will provide a great lesson for both new and seasoned investors - that the "free" market actually has more power than a managed market!

At some point, gold will be priced at a level where average investors will find it difficult to afford. Being uncomfortable with this situation, but not wanting to be left out, they will compare the price of gold to silver, decide that silver is the "better buy" and react accordingly. Given that silver is a much smaller market, plus the fact that most people fall into the category of coming into the precious metals only after huge momentum has developed, the silver market will literally explode upward in price.

That silver is in such high demand, since it is strong, malleable and ductile, provides an excellent rationale for investors to consider accumulating it. The key to big profits is to take those profits when they become significant, rather than let them fade away after a primary market top. Seeking to help as many investors as possible to not only accumulate sizeable profits, but also keep the majority of their winnings, is the primary reason David Smith and myself are taking the time to write another book about the silver market.

Silver is a superb conductor of electricity, conducts heat, and reflects light better than any other element. As you work your portfolio into the topping area for the metals, try not to let greed get in your way, and do not expect to hit the exact top of the market, because this is truly an amateur's way of looking at investing. We have a number of strategies for you to consider, in helping to managing your way through what may prove to be one of the greatest upside moves in precious metals' history.

CHAPTER 2

Is it different this time?

The coming 3rd and finally parabolic stage will end in the distribution to small, inexperienced new traders & investors who will be subject to blind greed and frenzied panic. **Florian Grummes**

In some ways, this major cyclical bull market in the precious metals is not new. However, in other aspects it truly *is* different. Why? Because this is the first time in recorded history when the demise of a one-world currency takes place. It will affect the entire world.

Some may ask, "But isn't a universal currency what the globalists are working to achieve?" This may be the case, but for practical purposes, the U.S. dollar - which is the reserve currency of almost every bank on the planet - is currently in essence the world's currency. Therefore, when it "fails" the repercussions will be felt by almost everyone. There will be no escape; daily life will change literally overnight as people adjust to different and largely unexpected circumstances.

A Titanic Undertaking

Certainly there are ways to mitigate these financial problems. The primary method of remaining financially insulated to the greatest degree is to hold real money, completely outside the banking and financial system. This is easily accomplished, yet at the present time, perhaps only one half of one percent of the population has actually achieved this all-important status.

Steve St. Angelo notes this fact:

> As precious metal analysts-investors bicker about whether THIS IS A SILVER SHORTAGE or not, the U.S. and the world move closer to the worst collapse in human history. This is actually much worse than musicians playing music on the Titanic as it sinks. Why? There were 713 survivors on the Titanic of the total 2,229 passengers and crew. Thus, 32% survived the sinking, whereas only 1-2% of investors (today) have gold and silver lifeboats.

There are several reasons for the lack of understanding about the importance of having - in your possession - fully paid for and readily available precious metals' coins. Coins - either bullion rounds or formerly circulating coins - which are accepted by nearly everyone, and that can be used anywhere in the world, may provide options to you that nothing else will.

First, it is so important for the Establishment to continue with the status quo on a global basis, that practically no mention of precious metals is ever made in the mainstream news outlets - financial or otherwise. When they do bring up the topic of gold (silver is almost never discussed), it is usually framed around some negative connotation.

The world is losing (con)fidence

We are facing the biggest risk to the monetary system ever recorded! Contrast this with the relatively small number of people who have some means of escaping it. Think about that!

The whole world is heading towards a huge dislocation, based upon a lack of trust in the banking/governmental system. The one financial asset with the most potential to help the greatest number is not even talked about outside the alternative media. This asset is held by the smallest ever percentage of people, which means that most of the population will have to suffer the consequences from their lack of knowledge.

It is extremely important to understand that in most cases, preserving real wealth alone may not be sufficient to insulate yourself and those you care about from the coming economic reset. First, while no one really knows exactly how the global economic unraveling will unfold, you can rest assured that it will vary somewhat, depending upon your location.

People from all walks of life will be affected. Possible exceptions might be the Amish, or some other community that is more or less self-sufficient and insulated from a heavily-dependent relationship on government - be it local, state or federal. This could also include elements in the Native American tribal environment, or perhaps Russian fur trappers in the Arctic.

In reality though, almost everyone will be impacted in significant ways. The general trend will be toward a lower standard of living. It could take a significant amount of time to bring things back to normal, which means that the "new normal" of lower living standards compared to the current metric could last a generation or more.

This time around, we could see a freeze up in peoples' ability to buy a significant amount of precious metals. For example if one of the major funds decided to add 20-30 million ounces of silver to their holdings, such a quantity would likely be unavailable, regardless of the price the fund was willing to pay.

However, it should be noted that these types of situations are **EXTREMELY RARE**. They only take place when already-obtained precious metals are held so tightly, due to the fear of what is taking place in the financial/monetary system, that almost no offer is good enough to cause a sizeable amount of metal to change hands. Yet we are convinced that this point in history, where such an extreme condition will be witnessed, lies just ahead of us.

Such an occurrence would exist for a very limited time. Whether or not it is probable, it is certainly possible! If this were to occur, it would ignite a surge of demand for the mining shares, which could turn into a frenzy. A "claim" on everything gold or silver would be sought after with a zeal not previously seen.

Confiscation?

Many people think that a confiscation is going to take place along the lines of what happened in the U.S. in the 1930's. We at *The Morgan Report* are of the opinion that it is highly unlikely the government will undertake to seize the public's precious metals holdings.

Given the manner in which they have consistently ridiculed gold all along the way as its price has ascended, it would discredit them, becoming proof-positive of their utter hypocrisy.

A much more likely event, would be passage of some type of huge "windfall profits" tax. This would place gold and silver bugs in a class warfare situation in relation to the lion's share of the population, who would be holding virtually no metal of their own. That majority could feel smug in their ignorance pertaining to real money in general, and precious metals in particular. They would most likely support the government's efforts to tax (confiscate) a great portion of the "windfall" profits legitimately earned by wise investors who had prepared ahead of time by exchanging some of their lawfully-earned "paper promises" for hard money.

This is another compelling reason why we think that diversifying into resource sector stocks is a wise and balanced move. The tax rate on gold and silver mining stock profits is likely to be treated just like earnings on stocks from any other market sector. And if your trading account is housed within the confines of a ROTH - which utilizes previously-taxed money to generate tax-exempt returns, then so much the better!

There are ways to legally limit your liability, if or when you decide to sell some or all of your precious metals holdings, and these will be addressed in future issues of our newsletter. One obvious but seldom discussed method, is to use your physical holdings as collateral for a loan. The loan rate could be structured at a point substantially lower than the tax rate. This type of action would have to be looked at later, in light of current tax rules, but for now, it provides a starting point for discussion.

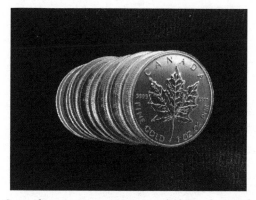

Canadian 1 troy ounce Gold Maple Leafs

Most stackers have a diverse collection of metals. There is some possibility that, at the market's top, a tube of Silver Eagles might sell for $1,000. Now granted, I (David Morgan) am NOT forecasting this price, just using it to illustrate a point! Imagine trying to get rid of a 100 ounce bar of silver, if the price was near the $500 per troy ounce level!

Silver bars of 100 troy ounces have been an efficient (and visually attractive) way to purchase metal over the past couple of decades, but that doesn't mean it will be easy to dispose of them when financial uncertainty peaks. Selling a 100 ounce bar might generate far too much attention. Thus a "small" unit transaction of a tube of silver rounds, a handful of "junk silver" (pre-1965 formerly circulating dimes, quarters or half-dollars), or just a single silver bullion coin - could offer the most flexibility when an investor is ready to capture profits.

Building liquidity - with your dealer

Another consideration for precious metals' investors this time around is liquidity. Building a strong relationship with your local metals' dealer(s) could be very useful when you wish to liquidate a portion, or all of your holdings. This could become an important element, given the very real possibility that some level of chaos might develop within the financial system.

Depending upon the conditions and state of affairs which come to exist, it might be worth a visit to the coin dealer every week or so, in order to sell some of your holdings. The size of the transaction would be dependent upon conditions at the time. New government regulations and taxing issues will certainly come into play. Again, we are simply looking ahead and asking ourselves how things "might be different this time."

Having been through the precious metals blow off in the spring of 1980, we believe it is important to remember that silver hit $50 for ONE DAY ONLY! Leading up to that final single day high, coin dealers literally had people lined up around the block, trying to sell their silver and gold.

In the Los Angeles area, every dealer got on the phone to "bid back" their buy price to $35 per ounce, when the futures price was $15 higher! Again, this was a one-time event and only lasted for a few days. This time around, however, we are not likely to see dealers lower their bid substantially below the spot market level.

First, because market participants these days are worldwide. Second, because industrial demand will also be competing with investors for physical silver. In fact, it's entirely possible that some desperate industrial users might even attach a premium to the spot price, in order to acquire the silver supplies necessary to meet their needs. At present, these users almost exclusively buy 1,000 ounce bars, but it's possible that they might be forced to make offers on name-brand 100 ounce bars as well.

In summary we do expect both gold, and especially silver, to get overvalued relative to what can be purchased in the marketplace. At the current time we plan to focus more on what a troy ounce of gold or silver will buy in terms of real estate, oil, a major stock index, an automobile or some other tangible good. Certainly, we will look at precious metals' pricing in terms of currency, but this may turn out to be a volatile measure during the events taking place in which the "top" is being achieved.

Rest assured, when the time comes to "cash in" on some or all of your precious metals investments, there will be so much personal and market emotion going on, that it will be extremely difficult to make a decision about selling. The tendency for most people will be to hold on for the lure of even higher prices. This will be the time when having accurately answered the questions we pose in this book as they relate to your personal circumstances and goals will be as important to your financial success as whether or not you "bought at the bottom" or about which hot mining stocks you had earlier purchased at "bargain" prices.

Are Mining Stocks Tomorrow's Blue Chip Equities?

If we take a look back in time to one of the most horrendous economic hardships ever faced in the United States -The Great Depression - we find that Homestake Mining and Dome Mines, were two gold producers that made their shareholders wealthy during those dark days. Before Barrick Gold acquired Homestake, I (David Morgan) used to be fond of stating, that from the initial Dow companies listings, Homestake was one of the few originals! In other words, gold and gold mining companies have truly stood the test of time.

Much of today's economic commentary revolves around a large contraction in the financial landscape, with the Baltic Dry Index hitting lows, some of the largest banks being basically insolvent, and even China's economy showing ominous signs of slowing down. Many financial commentators are looking for a possible recession, or even a deflationary period before the Central Banks can force currency into the system and kick-start inflation on Main Street.

At the peak in 1938, a $1,000 investment in Homestake grew to $6,760! However, this is only part of the story, because that was simply nominal growth, but during a deflationary period every "dollar" becomes more valuable as time goes on.

Moreover, during the next six years, Homestake Mining paid out a total of $128 in cash dividends. The 1935 dividend alone reached $56 per share. That's almost a 70% yield payout (basis 1929) in only one year! Indeed, hard asset investments (gold mining shares) were, as Jay Taylor phrases it, "islands of economic refuge during the grueling years of the Great Depression."

It was about gold prohibition...and revaluation.

We must remember that when gold was revalued (by FDR), margins for the gold miners exploded. It was hard to lose money when the newly hiked sales price was guaranteed and your costs were either stable or falling. It was an unexpected bonanza of gargantuan proportions. The Hearst family, who controlled the Homestake mine, rewarded themselves, and minority holders with much of this bounty via dividends. Today, it's hard to imagine any gold miner paying out the majority of its earnings this way. Nevertheless, rewarding shareholders with "handsome" dividends during the coming years is a distinct possibility.

So where does this put us today? First we need to clarify that gold is not only an inflation hedge, but also a crisis hedge. As the above example clearly illustrates, gold miners did extremely well during the 1930's depression. However, we need to realize the circumstance that helped bring these results about.

Though gold was revalued upward by Federal decree, people - also by Federal decree - could not legally own it. The mining producers started making large profits, while their operational costs remained fixed. So by default, gold shares became a proxy for owning gold. Thus the rush into mining stocks by the investing public, leading to a stunning rise in share prices, followed by large dividend payouts.

For those interested in this fascinating topic, Professor Roy Jastram's work *The Golden Constant* provides a unique examination of how gold's purchasing power has remained consistent over the centuries. This book is the only in-depth examination we know of that looks at how the purchasing power of gold has performed over the centuries in both England and the USA. It contains a thorough explanation of how the gold market evolved as it related to economic and political developments - dating from 1560 in England, and from 1800 in the USA. I can state without hesitation that academics, economic historians and economists interested in monetary and financial history will find his work to be extremely valuable.

What's not immediately evident, is that during much of that time frame, the world at large was on a gold standard, or at least had some tie to gold. Yet how do we analyze today's markets, which operate in terms of a system that currently has no tie to gold whatsoever? Do we need a different metric? Perhaps not.

There is still after all, a "constant".

Multiple examinations have determined that every time a "monetary system" read—currency - was not tied to real money (gold and/or silver), sooner or later that currency <u>always</u> failed. Without exception.

Yet, today we find that many (most?) in the academic and economic realm either insist this failure cannot take place, or that paper (currency) will trump gold. Supposedly - for the first time in recorded history - a piece of paper (digital or cloth) will reign supreme over a substance that for thousands of years has been revered and used as money. It must be stated that as we write this, authorities in a number of jurisdictions are implementing requirements banning, or at least discouraging, cash transactions, in favor of fully digital systems. (In fact, Sweden has almost completed its plan to "trash cash", by the prohibition of any and all financial activities involving the use of paper currency. This is just one facet of a concerted effort by the banking system at large, proceeding as quickly as possible, to ensure that paper wins over gold.

Is it different this time?

In certain ways it is different, because the looming failure of the world's reserve currency -the U.S. dollar - will affect nearly every person, business, bank, and financial institution on the planet. Meanwhile, the demand to escape the current financial breakdown is unlimited, when an asset class, precious metals, are sought by anyone and everyone who is motivated by the fear of losing their security - in a system that is falling apart before their eyes.

Every time in the past that this psychological shift in consciousness, from support of, to a loss of confidence in, the prevailing currency has taken place, the downward spiral has become swift and at some point, uncontrollable. Which means that all the propaganda from the mainstream press will have no effect in stopping a "run to gold."

It is quite possible that during the collision of new demand with very tight supply and strongly held positions in both gold and silver, additional purchases in size will become impossible. Large hedge funds, ETF's, Sovereign Wealth Funds, etc. will not be able to find precious metal in the quantity they desire, with the effect that prices will be bid to extremely high levels.

Every time there is a financial panic, fear drives the decision-making process, making clear judgment go out the window. If we truly witness a run to gold, it is highly likely that large gold dealers will decide to hold onto their inventory, and avoid transacting business until the currency markets stabilize.

All of this seems almost unimaginable, because it has rarely occurred in history. Since these outlier events usually skip generations, there is little "retained memory" by the people, of the hardships imposed by a system that pretends it can print wealth, when in fact true wealth must be produced through the activity conducted within a rational economic system, supported on a strong monetary foundation.

All of this leads to our belief that mining shares have the distinct potential of going into a once-in-a-lifetime bull market so extraordinary, that one like it has not been seen since the 1930's. It will be driven by the fact that when people cannot buy gold or silver, they will race to the mining shares, because of their belief that they serve as a proxy for physical gold and silver still in the ground.

Think about it... You run a large hedge fund and, ahead of your peer group, you can see what's coming. But as a stock-only restricted money manager - prohibited from buying commodities - you cannot legally buy physical gold. However, (and this is one reason why metals and miners' ETFs were created), you can still "obey the law" while holding a position in ETF gold and silver-like derivatives.

Back to the point, because there are so few top-tier precious metals companies, the amount of money flooding into these issues will take them to an extreme valuation. A wild card in all of this is that the cost of extraction is dependent upon several factors, with energy being the most important consideration. Therefore, profits could be compromised during a financial crisis, depending upon how the oil market behaves.

Regardless, the overall margins in the mining shares might become so unbelievable that the normal leverage of about three-to-one (miner performance versus gold/silver) could go to something like ten-to-one for the majors; well beyond that for mid-tier and junior miners.

Two Scenarios. In Either Case, Investors can Win. Big.

The real question to ask ourselves is what the financial landscape will look like after the initial panic into the precious metals, which could thereafter fuel an historic rise in the mining shares themselves.

If the move is parabolic and unsustainable, we would need to approach the situation with an in and out trading strategy. However, in my opinion, it is much more likely that the financial elite would be forced to implement gold backing into the monetary system (revaluating gold in relation to paper asset classes), with precious metals being revalued at a much higher level than at present.

This scenario would imply that mining share margins would remain elevated for quite awhile. Dividend payments would be sought after by income seekers, pension funds, insurance companies and many others. Over time, this investment class could change into a "utility" type of mentality with a real money (gold and silver) basis.

There is little doubt that, regardless of the outcome, the rise in precious metals that lies ahead of us will be historic in nature. Given my oft-stated belief, based upon extensive research, that as much as ninety percent of the profit in a major bull market can be achieved during the last ten percent of the time of that bull market's run, the implication, is that what lies ahead for the precious metals/miners may truly be one for the record books!

"Back up the Truck"

Now is the time to "back up the truck" in terms of your education on these topics, in order to acquire the best understanding possible of Mr. Market - and of yourself. Learn the important questions you need to answer ahead of time, as the second and more devastating financial tsunami builds and heads for shore.

Increasing the odds of achieving your financial goals will be all about understanding the market's tone, and of controlling your trading behavior and emotions.

Remember that in a major Bull Market, the function of the bull is to shake off as many participants as possible on its way to the ultimate top! This means that you need to hang on tight! The best way to do that is to buy relatively early and ride out all (but the last couple of) the scary corrections.

Buy right, then down the line, be willing and able to sell when you can - not when you must. Adding to what you already know - or suspect - in these areas, *Second Chance: How to Make and Keep Big Money During the Coming Gold and Silver Shock Wave* can add critical information to help in your decision-making process. *Adelante*!

CHAPTER 3

Keeping it Simple:
Insurance vs. Profit

> *At certain times in history owning money is the best available idea "investment" because all other investment classes have become so corrupted and distorted that having money is the only sensible choice. We are at such a point today, which means people that are the best informed choose to place a portion of their wealth into the precious metals....*
> **David Morgan**

The Japanese have a saying, "It's an ill wind that blows no good." When the financial tsunami shock-wave that's headed toward us engulfs the global economy, it will precipitate the greatest wealth-transfer in the history of humankind. Assets will move from one group - the unprepared, to another set of people - those who paid attention to the storm that was forming, and took appropriate action beforehand.

The same financial wave that will be so destructive to most asset classes also contains within it a parallel wave. This ground swell, based upon simple supply-demand metrics, will drive precious metals and mining stocks to levels many times higher than was the case in 2016. As an antidote to the collapse of an old financial order and the rise of a new one, this subset of the resource sector offers those who understand how to work with it, "sky high profit potential."

We believe it is extremely important to plan and execute the Insurance

17

leg of your strategy before you establish and begin to work on what may be the more exciting... and without a doubt, riskier element of your investment program. If you approach this project in the order we suggest, you will be accomplishing several important things.

First, by acquiring some "hold in your hand" precious metals, you will have established a financial underpinning that can help protect at least a portion of your overall monetary holdings. Gold and silver prices tend to move in a contrary manner to most other asset classes. When confidence falls, the economy struggles, inflation (or deflation) gets out of control, people tend to change their financial perspective. They move from what the trade calls "risk-on" assets like real estate, bonds, Treasury bills and the broader stock market, to a "risk-off" posture, wherein physical gold and silver are eagerly sought.

While you're at it, don't just think of precious metals as a "fear trade". They're also, as Frank Holmes has aptly framed it, a "love trade"- defined as the cultural affinity for precious metals by those living in China, India, SE Asia and the Middle East. Millions of *Chindians* (people from China and India) are buying gold and silver for dowries, jewelry, and "in the ground" savings accounts. Demand from these sources will push precious metals higher over the coming years, regardless of the level of stress in the financial system.

Second, while you (should) have established your gold and silver "stash" primarily as an "insurance policy", if the kind of price rise we foresee over the next few years comes to pass, you could also be looking at a substantial <u>profit</u> from your metals' holdings. Several independent analysts, and mining executives with strong predictive track records have publicly stated their belief that, before the geo-political and supply-demand imbalance crises we face have been resolved, gold could trade between $5,000 - $10,000, and silver, perhaps towards $400 per ounce. If an entirely possible silver/gold ratio of 25:1 were to occur... then plug in some price assumptions and do the math yourself. Chances are, you'll have a big grin on your face!

There's a Third aspect to establishing your own precious metals position. It has the ability to act as a counterweight to the "Profit" leg of your mining sector investment program - which in the next chapter we'll discuss in considerable detail. For now, let's just say that, should the Investment Leg underperform for some reason, the possibility of considerably higher prices for the physical metals you hold might end up providing a different kind of "insurance" for your profit-achieving efforts, as well as being a counterweight to the decline or destruction of value in the holdings of more traditional assets. We can now discuss how you might establish an insurance position.

Let's get physical

Almost from the time I (David Morgan) penned the first issue of my newsletter, *The Morgan Report*, we have advised subscribers to start their program by first acquiring physical gold and silver. The primary idea is that you begin with having "hold in your hand" physical metal - upon which by definition, no one else but you has claim.

As to what percentage of one's investible funds should be devoted, there is really no "one size fits all" approach. Briefly and simply stated, opinions on this subject run from 5% - 25% (In the TMR Ten Rules of Silver Investing, we have stated 10%). Suffice it to say that you should thoroughly think through just how confident you are about the precious metals' bull market thesis, what your temperament can handle in relation to the market's well-known volatility, and how you want to fit a physical metal's percentage holding into the overall matrix of your insurance, investment, and planning outlook.

For most of us, owning physical metals is going to mean holding "coins", but usually not "collectible" ones. Save this venue for the serious student of numismatics - someone who is both knowledgeable plus willing and able to accept a much different type and level of risk than the rest of us should even consider taking upon ourselves. Not to confuse the issue, but a person may, on occasion, want to "break this rule" by purchasing a particular "investment grade" coin that they simply just love to have.

An exception I made several years ago - at David Morgan's suggestion - was to start a collection of American Silver Eagle Bullion Coins - one for each year they have been minted, going back to 1986, and adding another one for each successive year the U.S. Mint continues to produce them. For this special set, which will be willed to my children, the goal was to collect encapsulated professionally-evaluated coins, graded from MS 65 - 70. The one for early 2016, an MS 70, cost me $55. At the time, spot silver was $15. An ungraded Silver Eagle would have only cost about $18, or $3 over spot. You can see by this example that I paid "a lot more than I had to", but with a specific and well-thought out reason, and into which was allocated only a small amount of investible funds.

A lady bought gold, saw prices triple, yet lost two-thirds of her money.

One particularly heart-rending story came to us by way of a good friend. He is an investment letter writer and owner of a bullion sales business. In early 2011, an elderly lady came to him with a collection of gold coins she wanted to have appraised and sold. Several years earlier, from another dealer, she had simply tried to buy a quantity of gold bullion. But rather than sell her the type of gold vehicle we'll discuss shortly, she was talked into buying "collectibles".

She dropped over $1 million dollars on those coins, at a time when gold was going for about $500 a troy ounce. When she came into our friend's establishment, the metal was more than $1,500, so she should have been able to sell her hoard for $3 million dollars - tripling her original investment. But since the premiums on many of the coins she had been convinced to buy were grossly inflated, her collection was now appraised at only $300,000. She had managed to lose two-thirds of her original investment! Please do not let this happen to you!

Holding sensibly-priced bullion rounds and ingots is an important aspect of your financial insurance program, which can help protect a portion of your other assets from the depredations of inflation and asset destruction.

While not meant to be a comprehensive list, suggestions mentioned later in this chapter, purchased from legitimate dealers at a reasonable premium over the spot (cash) price, with a portion of your investible/ insurance-earmarked funds, should stand you in good stead. "Buying right" will help you get the most metal for your money, and enable you to sell some back, down the line when/if you decide to do so.

When you sell, you won't recoup the premium paid upon purchase. Generally, gold bullion can be sold back at or near the quoted spot price. Silver *may* sell back at spot as well. But since it is also an industrial metal, it's possible that during times of high redemption, the price you're being offered may be temporarily below spot. We remember, during the January - March 1980 silver topping process, that when spot was quoted at the mid-$40 level, commercial buyers were only paying retail sellers in the mid-$30 range. This was a temporary event and not nationwide, but it occurred often enough in major cities that we are obligated to mention it. By shopping around, you could find a difference of several dollars per ounce on the bid price! The watchword here is to be intentional when you buy... and when you sell.

OWNx Gold-Silver Savings Program

For those silver and gold stackers who save in precious metals on a regular basis, we have found a program that is safe, easy and secure. In effect, the consistent saver is practicing a form of dollar cost averaging, buying automatically, without regard to the up and down swings of precious metals' prices. A person may choose to buy a specified dollar amount monthly, weekly, bi-weekly, or even daily. Your metals are allocated and you may take delivery if/as desired. This monthly program is also suitable for one time or random purchases. http://preciousmetalssavingsprogram. com I (David Morgan) have known the founders for a number of years.

Make sure what you buy is real!

Counterfeit coins, bullion rounds and ingots have begun finding their way into the market, to the detriment of more than a few hapless buyers. Many of these fakes - some rather sophisticated, are sourced from China.

Regardless of their origin, you don't want to become a victim. From whom you buy should always be an issue of paramount concern, before you lay your Benjamins, Grants, and Jacksons on the counter. CoinWeek.com provides a clear summation, stating:

> These new fakes not only have a better strike quality than previous examples, but there are no obvious errors in the packaging which bears the certificate number and other authentic-looking details from the purported manufacturer. Measure the fake by length and width, and it seems like the real deal, but the bars are noticeably thicker when compared to a genuine bar, so that these fake PAMP Suisse gold bars weigh the same as the real thing.
>
> The most important step is to make sure you're buying from a reputable, licensed dealer. Some people buy from established local sellers they've dealt with for years. Others only purchase from big well-known precious-metal dealers on the Internet...

The main point is to make sure you know with absolute certainty who you're buying from. Does the firm have a vested interest in carefully screening what it buys and sells? Will you have recourse if it turns out what you bought isn't the real deal? The counterfeiters are getting better and better at what they do. The only way to combat them is to be a smart buyer of authentic gold coins and bars.

They're not just talking about "collectibles" either. There's big money to be made by unscrupulous sellers in garden-variety bullion rounds and bars too. Nowadays, in addition to *caveat emptor*, it's *caveat venditor* (seller beware)!

Be careful of buying from a source advertising from popular online merchandising sites like eBay and Craig's List. Even if a seller has a lot of "likes" around his/her ads, the potential for not getting quite what you thought you paid for still exists.

ALSO, seldom buy from a precious metals' ad you see in the Sunday paper, or from a flyer that turns up in your mail box. If you find yourself waiting for extended delivery times, seek to resolve the issue as soon as possible and consider whether you ought to do business with that source again. There are times when delivery delays are legitimate, but this seldom happens when you're dealing with an established seller who has deep connections in the metals' supply chain, and who regularly meets their customer's expectations.

An instructive - and luckily not too costly learning incident was recounted recently by a friend. As soon as he began describing his experience, it was apparent what the outcome was going to be! He had seen an ad in a magazine for bags of "unsorted, formerly-circulating precious coins." Since supposedly, no one had looked through them, the idea was that "Gee, maybe there could be something of exceptional value in those bags!" Well, after paying a steep price, receiving his supposed-treasures in the mail, and sorting through them, he of course found nothing of the kind. Do you really think someone is going to send you grab-bags of coins they have not looked though first?

In the last few years, several nationally-known precious metals' dealers have gone bankrupt. In each case, there was something systemically wrong with their business model. They may not have been properly hedged against market volatility - after previously taking the customers' money. They may have been speculating in the highly-leveraged futures market in excess of their hedging needs. They may have even been using the business' cash flow as a personal ATM to fund their own lifestyles. Taking a "draw" on your business - especially when it involves dipping into the customer's funds on deposit - is always highly questionable. In these circumstances, the client's funds may be at risk.

As gold and silver move into new all-time nominal highs, expect every caveat we've discussed to become a more common and pronounced situation in the marketplace minefield. Just another reason to be extremely careful when you're "in the market" for some precious metal. Research carefully before you lay down a single "paper promise." Start with a small purchase. Then if something goes wrong, you have only risked a small amount.

Don't wait until the public mania kicks in, to get what you need for financial protection. Fund your program sooner rather than later. After it has become "obvious" to more and more of your friends and neighbors that what you've been saying and acting upon all along is coming to pass, you can sit back and watch them scurry around trying to do what you've already accomplished. (As an additional caveat, it's a good idea to keep you metals' purchase and storage locations to yourself. Tell a family member and let it go at that. You don't need a stranger showing up in the middle of the night at your house to "make a withdrawal.")

Gold or Silver?

It's best in almost all cases to have both metals. Gold is far less volatile than silver, and so compact that most people can put a whole year's wages in the front pocket of their jeans. Silver has far more potential for outsized gains, but is "bulky" relative to gold.

For gold, consider the one troy ounce American Gold Eagle, Canadian Gold Maple Leaf, South African Krugerrand, or the American Gold Buffalo - a less durable coin for carry-around use due to its almost totally pure (.9999) gold content. There are others of course - such as the Austrian Philharmonic coin. Some of these used to be circulating currency, based upon face value. However, a knowledgeable person would not consider exchanging a one ounce $50 gold piece for...$50 dollars, knowing that an ounce might be going for fifteen hundred - or at some point, several thousand dollars.

If you'd like proof that there *are* a lot of clueless people out there, go to Youtube and find examples of people on the street who were offered a one ounce gold or silver coin at some ridiculously-low price. In almost every case they just weren't interested. When given the choice of a candy bar or the coin, they always took the candy. In one pathetic case, a young lady would not even trade her partially-consumed iced tea... for a 10 ounce silver bar!

Another reason to buy recognized (especially gold) coins is because the likelihood of deception becomes less of a concern. Buying from an established dealer - and purchasing U.S. Mint or Perth Mint-generated coins should keep you on the safe side.

A side-bar is to consider holding fractional ounce gold bullion rounds. One half, one quarter and one-tenth troy ounce rounds are easily acquired. One-tenth ounce gold is a bit on the tiny side - smaller than a U.S dime, so you might want to stick with the one-quarter and one-half ounce sizes.

1 troy ounce American Gold Buffalo

Silver options: Fractional ounces and formerly-circulating "money"

Before 1965, U.S. coinage in dimes, quarters and half dollars were minted with 90% silver. This changed the following year, with only Kennedy Half Dollars - now known as "clads" still being minted with 40% silver. By 1970, no circulating U.S. coin being minted that year or later contained silver.

Nowadays, you'll be lucky to find one silver dime a year in the coins received when you buy something - proof positive of Gresham's Law, which states that "bad money drives out good." And by the way, that pre-1965 Washington Quarter you may stumble upon has a silver worth, at $22 an ounce - of about $4.00!

These coins - known in the trade as "junk silver" are packaged in canvas bags, and may have volatile premiums, depending upon supply-demand as well as the amount of silver price volatility. You can find a column which we wrote, discussing this topic with the title "Junk Silver is Not Junk" at moneymetals.com You may not be able to afford a full bag of $100 face value dimes quarters or halves - which at $20 silver spot will cost you around $2,000. But you can buy a handful at most coin stores to meet your budget, no matter how limited it might be.

Plata pura en la mano
(courtesy Money Metals Exchange)

The case for owning formerly-circulating gold coins

Interesting - and functional -choices for a fractional, formerly-circulating coin are the British Sovereign (which has .2354 troy ounces of gold content) or the 1 mm smaller Swiss Gold 20 Franc (at .1867 oz actual gold weight) At a $1,300 spot gold price, you will pay around $350 for a Sovereign and about $275 for a Swiss 20 Franc. The fractional premiums are somewhat more on a relative basis than for a full ounce of gold. When touring a foreign country, you might choose to carry a few as pocket change. If your wallet or purse is stolen, you would be able to take your coins to a reputable coin shop or many banks virtually anywhere in the world, and exchange them for currency to purchase a plane ticket or lodging.

Gold and Silver are a financial source of liquidity, which if needed can be disposed of easily and safely. They can be used as an alternative form of payment to the "paper promises" - un-backed (fiat) paper money in your wallet or purse. In effect it's real, "hard" money. And unlike real estate, most collectibles and other large valuable items, it's portable.

You __MUST__ buy from reputable and fairly-pricing dealers.

It helps to "shop locally" where you can speak face to face with a knowledgeable coin/bullion dealer having an established reputation. If that's not feasible, search out a nationally-known, highly-rated dealer - one who either mints gold and/or silver bullion rounds and coins, or who buys the finished product from a private mint. A few mining companies mint 1 troy ounce .999 fine silver rounds with their logo emblazoned on the obverse.

We're not fans of buying from unknown parties online - who may or may not be as much on the up and up as ones you can locate after a moderate amount of due diligence.

A few thoughts on what you should look for when it comes to buying precious metals from a distant locale. First, go to their website, and read everything therein carefully. If/when you decide to call, your questions should be answered politely and promptly.

A salesperson should never try to "up-sell" you into purchasing "collector coins", "first strike" specimens, "graded-coins" or "limited editions." If you think about it, ALL coins and rounds are "limited" quantity, are they not? Otherwise, the production run would have to continue indefinitely! The premium over "spot" - the physical price for which the metal is trading at the time, should not be excessive. But as prices rise into the stratosphere, the premium will definitely rise along with it.

One approach with which we are familiar is conducted by <u>Resource Consultants</u> in Tempe, AZ. Their "Gold Category One - Insurance" recommends gold and silver bullion coins and bars; "Category Two - Insurance with a Kicker" offers gold coins, such as the $20 St. Gaudens, which were once used as money in the U.S. Their "Category Three - Speculation" recognizes that some people may be attracted to own a few of the more volatile third-party graded U.S. numismatic, common date gold coins, which can move, in either direction, considerably more than the underlying spot price of the bullion they contain.

Any dealer with which you do business should provide clarity about what they offer, answer your questions fully before you've committed funds, and not pressure you into buying more or different products than you want. Upon placing an order and the funds to pay for it as per their requirements, prompt delivery to you by insured mail should be expected.

Coming to your Inbox soon. Beware! - Two real-life examples we have received

This was a "cold call" email from Croatia. Any red flags here?

Dear Sirs,
We urgently needs (sic) higher amounts of gold bars, nougat (sic) or dast(sic). Buyer from Belgium. As (sic) a guarantee of payment opens escrow account. Accepts all quantities…The procedure we can start immediately.

- Aleksandar Ruski, Zagreb, Croatia

This uninvited guest touted a hot mining stock: (We've relabeled the company name "SCAM".)

"SCAM" Breaking News

Fellow Investor,

We are very excited that SCAM has announced they will explore their properties with the intention of starting to drill... SCAM shares have the potential to jump 1,861% during the coming year... from less than $1 to $8.04, or beyond.

You missed your chance to get SCAM for less than $0.60. Once shares break out, things are going to move fast. Dont (sic) miss your last opportunity to buy SCAM for less than $1.00!

Our advice: Read the Disclaimer, or better yet - Just say "Delete".

The "Monster Box"

The American Silver Eagle is a beautiful one-troy ounce specimen produced by the U.S. Mint, and sold to the retail market through dealers who purchase directly from the Mint.

These .999 fine beauties, usually sold in Brilliant Uncirculated (BU) condition, generally carry a $3+ premium over spot. They can be had as singles, 25 to a roll tubes, or in "monster boxes" of 500 coins (20 x 25). If you buy a Monster Box, it's good to keep it sealed with the straps provided by the Mint, since most coin dealers - for obvious reasons -will offer a higher trade-in value if the box has remained unopened.

U.S. Mint Silver Monster Boxes are shipped to over 50 countries around the globe. They weigh over 40 pounds apiece, so if you're buying several, you may want to literally "back up the truck" to lug them home.

This description from monsterbox.com sums up their advantages nicely:

> "Monster boxes can be purchased sealed or unsealed. An unsealed box generally means the contents have been swapped out or removed for other purposes. Unsealed monster boxes tend to be cheaper than their sealed counterparts due to the likelihood that its 500 coins have been fully or partially replaced by coins that were not minted together. As far as quality and collectors

are concerned, a sealed monster box always represents a homogenous group of 500 coins certified under one label. Unsealed boxes can contain coins mixed and matched from another set and therefore demand a lower premium."

The Canadian Mint makes a "monster box" with 20 x 25 to a tube, "four nines" (.9999 fine) Canadian Silver Maple Leafs having a $5 face value, as does the Austrian Mint. Australia's Perth Mint now sells a 250 count "Mini-Monster box" of 1 troy ounce Silver Kangaroos having a total weight of around 22 pounds.

Perth Mint 1 troy ounce Silver Kangaroos

If you wait until the public mania phase heats up, you may still be able to purchase a monster box, but it could look like this...

Empty Monster Box

There's no substitute for physical!

Yes, you could consider trading/investing in mining stocks and ETFs, and no, you should not consider them as substitutes for first acquiring some physical gold and silver. It doesn't matter that several high-profile billionaires, apparently as a way to protect (hedge) their portfolios, have taken major positions in gold Exchange Traded Funds (ETFs). This may turn out to be false reasoning on their part, as Bullion Management Group's Nick Barisheff notes:

Their investments in ETFs may ultimately negate the very reason for investing in gold in the first place. Only physical gold provides true diversification outside of the financial system. Physical gold is immune from counterparty risk or liquidity constraints. Investing in gold proxies may work under normal conditions for short-term trades and hedging strategies, but will be subject to the same systemic risks that financial assets will incur. The time when you need the protection of gold the most is the time when these proxies are most likely to fail and not provide the portfolio protection of bullion owned directly.

No less a source than the Bank of International Settlements (BIS) has weighed in on this topic, saying,

Crisis experience has shown that as the intermediation chain lengthens, it becomes complicated to assess the risks of financial products due to lack of transparency as to how risks are managed at different levels of the intermediation chains. Exchange-traded funds, which have become popular among investors seeking exposure to a diversified portfolio of assets, share this characteristic, especially when returns are replicated using derivative products. As the volume of such products grows, such replication strategies can lead to a build up systemic risks in the financial system.

We'll discuss the pros and cons of ETFs in a future chapter. The key takeaway now is to understand that the primary reasons for owning physical metal and the rationale for investing in ETFs and mining stocks are entirely different. Even if you believe - as we do - that all three categories offer significant upside potential going forward, they are categorically different in terms of acquisition strategy, price appreciation potential, anticipated end use, and risk.

Follow-on shock-waves from the 2008 malfeasance are "written in the rocks"

Second Chance began with the premise that, as a result of unresolved financial issues left over from the global near-disaster of 2008 when the first financial tsunami struck, we are now set up for a repeat impact, only this time much worse, as the follow-on shock wave hits the entire planet's economic system during the next few years. Not only have the original systemic shortfalls <u>not</u> been addressed, but in almost all cases they've gotten considerably worse.

Lest we think that anyone in the IMF's dysfunctional hall of mirrors has even seen the dots, let alone connected them, a report from the IMFs own internal audit department should disabuse that notion. The Daily Telegraph's Ambrose Evans-Pritchard sums it up clearly in one tight paragraph, remarking that,

> The International Monetary Fund's top staff misled their own board, made a series of calamitous misjudgments in Greece, became euphoric cheerleaders for the euro project, ignored warning signs of impending crisis, and collectively failed to grasp an elemental concept of currency theory.

Apparently the central bankers forgot that capital formation - via savings, not the printing press, is what stimulates sustainable economic growth. When they inject money - digital or paper - into the system, there is a tendency for it to flow initially to where its owners believe they'll get the best return. It may be productive, such as starting a new business, but most likely it goes to the Protected Class at the top, wherein it heads into such dubious activities as company share buybacks, government debt (bonds) purchases, establishment of derivatives, real estate speculation, influence peddling and other venues, most of which serve to distort, rather than strengthen the system.

In a moment of public candor rare for an autocrat, European commission president, Jean-Claude Juncker, said words to the effect that European politicians actually know how to solve the problems, but then afterwards they wouldn't be able to figure out how to get re-elected!

Due to the blind men (and women) leading the world's central banks, most notably the U.S. Federal Reserve - with Europe's minions and the IMF angling to be contenders, a new and even more virulent pestilence - zero interest rate (ZIRP) and negative interest rate (NIRP) policies... literally for the first time in recorded history - have been unleashed upon the world's economies. The idea is to force people to spend money in order to stimulate the economy. The result has been to render invisible, the signals usually given off by interest rates in helping market participants determine the wisdom of pursing a given economic enterprise or activity. Assumptions on investment return made by pension fund managers (now underfunded by as much as $8 trillion) and life insurance companies, not to mention retirees relying on interest from bonds to help offset inflation, are now being called into serious question.

On an individual/group basis, people are responding to a lack of yield by taking on more risk in stock market, real estate and "collectibles" speculations. The rules for money market funds are changing so that "breaking the buck" - keeping the net asset value of a share at no lower than $1, thus protecting the account's principle - will no longer be inviolate. Add to this, the subjective imposition of 'liquidity fees' 'redemption gates' and 'temporary halts on redemptions', while earning next to no interest from funds on deposit, and you have to wonder why anyone would keep even a base metal dime in a money market, rather than placing at least a portion of their account into some silver ones.

Another almost totally unrecognized negative from NIRP, is that banks are also having to "reach for yield." So they offer loans to less reliable customers, thereby weakening their balance sheets.

Distrustful of the banking system, and unwilling to pay the bank for the privilege of having a savings account, more people - and businesses - are beginning to hoard cash outside the system, and increasingly, turning to gold and silver for an enhanced level of security, protection of capital, and privacy from increasingly intrusive and dictatorial governments. Evidence of this in Europe is becoming more pronounced by the week.

This is all well and good for "early responders" to the klaxon call of the precious metals - which for thousands of years have been accepted across cultures and historical time-frames as real money. But soon there's going to be a problem. Declining gold and silver production, slammed by demand shock-waves from investors and average citizens of all nationalities - and yes, even central banks - will leave the supply cupboard increasingly bare, driving the price of what's left to buy, higher and higher.

Mining Stocks as the ultimate non-gold and silver "investment" vehicle.

As the supply of precious metal dries up and comes close to disappearing, those who desire to become involved in the resource sector will increasingly be driven into mining stocks, and variations on this theme - Exchange Traded Products (ETP/ETFs). This is where the investor who wishes to take his/her involvement in the sector "to the next level" - in terms of profit potential and risk - will likely find themselves.

CHAPTER 4

Catch and Ride the Wave...

The Western gold community is now entering the year 2016, as gold approaches another mighty support zone, this time at $1033. It's unknown whether gold enters that support zone, or rallies from just above it. What is known is that this is a major buying area, and a generational low appears to be in the works for both the bullion and the miners. Intestinal fortitude, and nurturing of investor spirit, are all that is required now. **Stewart Thomson**

One of the primary reasons so many investors don't come close to their financial goals, is that they haven't mapped out what they want to accomplish and how they intend to do it.

The Three-Legged Investment Stool

After many years of trial and error - and seeking to learn from those mistakes - I (David Smith) have settled upon a process that helps at the outset to lay the groundwork for a successful financial campaign. Before the first trade is ever made, an investor who sets things up this way and adapts it to his/her own "style" will find the odds of success greatly enhanced.

Catch the Wave...

The First Leg: Understand, Implement, and Flow with the Boyd Cycle

The most valuable Big Picture insights you're likely to run across will come from studying and applying the teachings of a man whose bio doesn't indicate that he ever spent much time in the investment world. Nevertheless, he may have inadvertently discovered and developed, for those willing to pay attention and modify it for their own use, a priceless investment tool! His name is John Richard Boyd.

Boyd was an Air Force fighter pilot in the Korean War, and later a consultant to the Pentagon. He was instrumental in the design and development of the F-16 fighter, and is credited with developing the successful strategy for the invasion of Iraq during the first Gulf War (1991).

His ideas revolutionized military theory and practice. His philosophy was first formalized while he was an instructor at TOPGUN. He observed air combat between opposing jet fighters over Korea, and reached the conclusion that the critical factor in responding to an event was *time*.

In what so often becomes the survival of the fittest in warfare - in markets, as well as in life – Boyd noted that *"The pilot who goes through the OODA cycle in the shortest time prevails because his opponent is caught responding to situations that have already changed."*

How the OODA Loop helps us as Investors

John Boyd's OODA Loop
(Courtesy Steven A. Smith)

His cycle – which continually resets itself - consists of four overlapping elements: Observe, Orient, Decide, and Act. In application, the pilot who was able to move through this circuit with the greatest precision and the most speed, won.

Simple, straightforward, repeatable. It's interesting how many people use only one or two of these 4 critical steps. In order to enhance your ability to ride the precious metals' and mining stocks' shock-wave successfully, you need to do all four... in order!

Observe – Get the Big Picture, economically, social and politically. How might an unexpected event like the UK Brexit vote or a collapse in Italy's government move the dial on demand for metals and miners? As a corollary, use knowledge filters to manage the influx of data, so you don't become overwhelmed. Ask yourself, "When do I have enough information to take action?" Since you never have all the necessary data, at some point you've got to make that final leap based upon intuition, experience, and gut feel.

In *Science, Strategy and War: The Strategic Theory of John Boyd*, Francis Osinga sums this up well, saying that "even if one has perfect information it is of no value if it is not coupled to a penetrating understanding of its meaning, if one does not see the patterns. Judgment is key. Without judgment, data means nothing. It is not necessarily the one with more information who will come out victorious, it is the one with better judgment, the one who is better at discerning patterns."

An analytical refinement aligning with Boyd's concepts - what Jim Rickards calls the "Kissinger Cross", seeks to enable accurate decision-making, where incomplete (but sufficient from a probability standpoint) knowledge intersects with the time remaining before an event takes place. Consider researching how Jim goes about this.

Orient – Next, ask yourself, "How do *I* fit into this picture?" Do my financial goals, ability to invest, belief structure, willingness to keep learning about the precious metals and miners, and risk tolerance (temperament) mesh with the volatile nature of these markets? Am I fully committed to the assumptions I hold? Or am I doing this only because a "guru" recommends it? If you half-heartedly believe the metals and mining stocks have a great future, then your efforts - and results will be half-hearted. Never stop orienting. As Boyd says, "Orienting isn't just a state you're in; it's an ongoing process. You're always orienting."

Decide – Lay out your plan. Ideally begin by establishing a physical stack of "hold in your hand" gold and silver. Start a dollar-cost averaging buy plan? Monthly/quarterly? How much do you want to commit? Then research/select a small number of high quality producers, and one or two near-to- production explorers. Consider holding at most, two dozen companies. Decide how to establish your positions. We favor buying in portions - *tranches*. Keep a single choice under 10% of your account. Better yet is 4%. Strive to hold a 10-15% cash reserve.

Act! – Once you've concluded the decision-making part of the cycle, get your program going. As you practice these steps - up to and including this one - you'll improve at going through the loop to reach the action step more quickly - and effectively. Sharpen and subtly refine this 4-step meta-tool, which holds out the possibility of increasing your trading success and profits... geometrically.

For establishing a physical position, carefully choose a legitimate bullion dealer with a proven track record, as well as a lot of satisfied customers, and embark upon your purchase schedule. Focus on what you're doing and don't let uninformed opinions or nay-sayers cause a diversion from your course of action. Don't forget the powerful and indispensable role the mind plays in your investment success. As "Mr. Gold" Jim Sinclair says, "Technique without a mindset is like a race car without fuel."

Accumulate in thirds or fifths into weakness whenever possible.

One-third now to establish the position, another third on a decline of 20% from the initial price. Go for a final third with a "stink bid", that may or may not ever be activated. Even highly liquid stocks can be negatively impacted by a misinterpreted geopolitical event, or a brokerage house "fat finger". It's also common for the best stocks to drop temporarily when a new financing is announced. If your Limit/GTC (good 'til cancelled) order is in place, you might get an intraday downdraft fill, and have a profit by the close!

In the next two chapters we'll discuss how to go about setting up a portfolio that can give you the potential of turning each dollar invested into 10... or more, as the last phase of this secular mega-market moves into the leading edge of a public mania.

It's fairly common for investors to do a good job working through the first three steps -or at least the observe/decide portions - of the OODA Loop, but then have a hard time taking ACTION!. These people even less frequently carry out the second step, Orienting. Since they've never looked inward too deeply, they let fear, doubt, or lack of focused attention rob them of what might have been a very successful trade. Not to mention the possibility of an entire investing campaign that could have handed them life-altering gains - the kind we believe we're in the formative stages of being generated right now.

No matter how you approach this subject, it's important to understand that Boyd's insights offer, in effect a learning system. Working the OODA Loop can help you more successfully deal with uncertainty and an always unknown future. Not just in the investment realm, but on the street, or with just about anything else that goes on in your life, where speed, accuracy, mindset, and an ability to adopt to changing circumstances are important - helping your mind to run as an open system, rather than a cloistered one.

John Boyd's theorems enable you to survey the landscape, look inside yourself and correlate the two. As you research and form a trading program composed of the elements necessary to conduct your own "campaign" on the investment battlefield, you achieve clarity and certitude in order to successfully execute your plans.

When all is said and done, and the day comes when you've decided to say "Good bye Mr. Market", utilizing the OODA Loop increases the likelihood you'll get out with the majority of your financial, emotional and physical skin intact. Let John Boyd's spirit be your talisman.

Like the perfect cast that softly places a dry fly just ahead of a trophy Leopard Rainbow trout feeding on a summer hatch in a clear, cold Alaskan stream, as the poised angler sets the hook with the proper pressure at just the right moment.

Like getting inside the Market's "loop" to ride this precious metals' bull run for a long as possible, extracting the maximum amount of profit from the positions you've established... and getting out "a bit early".

The Second Leg: Study and Apply both Fundamental <u>and</u> Technical Analysis

You'll succeed as an investor/trader to the extent that you come to terms with the two primary approaches to resource sector market analysis - Fundamental Analysis, and Technical Analysis. Becoming functionally competent in these two areas enables you, over time, to establish a portfolio of quality mining stocks and ETPs. You'll conduct well-thought out trades on satellite positions, taking profits off the table into great strength, and attempting to buy back some or all of those shares into temporary weakness.

The first of these disciplines, Fundamental Analysis, can be dispensed with fairly quickly, but getting the correct read at the outset improves your success as you move into the next approach, Technical Analysis.

Looking at Fundamentals – Supply/demand factors give you a sense of whether the item you're following is judged to be in surplus or deficit, what factors might alter this relationship, and how pricing dynamics in the marketplace may be reflected due to these changes.

Supply: For silver, pay attention to the annual global production figures from <u>The Silver Institute</u>. For gold, consider the <u>World Gold Council</u>. For each metal, you can also find a listing of the top tier producer countries and the amount of metal they mine.

Demand: Physical movement on the <u>Shanghai Gold Exchange</u> (trading Au, Ag, Pt), the COMEX, American Silver and Gold Sales from the U.S. Mint, Perth Mint (Australia). The Silver Institute details global silver consumption. Excellent updating resources to consider are the writings of <u>Koos Jansen</u> and <u>Steve St. Angelo</u>.

In a very real sense, demand "makes the charts", not the other way around. Initially a surge of buying on the COMEX can get a trend underway, but if the supply of a commodity or metal is burdensome and demand lackluster, at some point that trend is going to move in the opposite direction. Consider the fundamental back story as the "setup" by which chart patterns begin to form in support of it.

David Morgan states this truism, still relevant - if not more so - than when he first made it:

> ***Markets move on demand; whether that demand is industrial or investment means little to the market – <u>demand is the real driver</u>.***

If we focus on silver, it's important to note that in recent years, interest from investors is what has really put this metal on the map. Even though industrial demand is the larger segment of the pie, it's *investment* demand which has the potential to upset the supply apple cart and launch silver prices on a journey into outer space. We're now also starting to see indications of concern on the industrial side about reliable supply, should the tectonic plates of increasing silver investor desire and decreasing global production continue to rub against each other the wrong way.

Regarding the likelihood that these opposing forces could at some point bring about a price explosion, Ted Butler's comment seems particularly relevant. He says,..."the highly unique dual demand feature in silver –a vital industrial commodity and a universal investment asset – gives silver something not present in any other commodity, the possibility of a demand surge capable of creating a physical shortage."

2016 research from several sources has since revised the data for silver production during the last decade, concluding that silver supply *vis á vis* investment demand was in deficit for much of the time. We won't take space here to inform or try to convince you of the details - easily researched on the Internet. What we will state without equivocation, is that if as we suspect, silver investor interest from around the globe continues to advance, follow-on panic-like buying from industrial sources may be added to the mix. Fueled by unsteady production output, the available supply of silver to meet this aggregate demand - <u>when it is needed</u> - is going to continue under mounting, and at some point explosive pressure.

Yes, at some time after the blow-off top has been registered, a new silver supply-demand equilibrium will reassert itself, with prices for the metal declining sharply from whatever elevated point has been reached. But in our considered opinion, the height from which prices will fall, will have printed an historic figure in nominal <u>and</u> inflation-adjusted terms well into three digits.

Technical Analysis: Candlesticks?

Technical analysis attempts to divine the future price of a commodity or stock by looking at what the subject under review has done in the past. The discipline has a long history, dating back at least as far as 18th century feudal Japan, when rice merchants traded their wares by looking at price patterns of visuals called Candlesticks. As far as we know, the source credited with bringing an understanding of Candlesticks to Western traders is Steve Nison, who the story goes, learned it from a Japanese broker. Like bar charts, which we'll discuss shortly, the common Candlestick represents one day, showing the daily range of a stock or commodity, detailing its opening price, its high, low and close. A white body (wick) indicates a higher close than the open. A black (or red) body signals the daily close was lower than the open. These colors allow you to quickly judge market sentiment - bullish or bearish.

Weekly $Silver Candlesticks (Courtesy StockCharts.com)

A number of sources about this approach are available to give you a solid understanding. We are agnostic about Candlesticks. In short, we feel that while their study and practice have merit - like other forms of charting - using them successfully is as much an art as a science. Indeed, Candlesticks, in conjunction with the more commonly-used bar charts, might demonstrate that the two disciplines complement each other! No matter what charting approach you use, keep in mind that Mr. Market does not tend to pay attention to them him or herself. A key determinant of a trend's tidal direction is simply market "sentiment" - the ebb, flow, and sometimes flood - of fear, greed, stupidity, and occasionally, indifference, by the collective psyche of market participants. Therefore, you should regard Candlesticks or any other form of TA as *a* tool, not *the* tool in your trading kit.

Bar Charts?

Daily Open-High-Low-Close bar chart

It's safe to say that the majority of chartists today follow the discipline of bar charting as outlined in what has come to be known as the "bible" of technical analysis. Titled *Technical Analysis of Stock Trends*, it was originally published in 1948 by Robert Edwards and John Magee, later modernized by W.H.C. Bassetti. This 600 page tome gives the most die-hard TA freak a banquet of information from which to choose. Attempt to assimilate all of it if you must.

Regardless of the time being measured - daily, weekly, monthly or yearly, the bar chart has a high-low-close, and usually an open. The open has a short line off the bar to the left; the close has a short line to the right.

Endeavour Silver Weekly bar chart

There are many "indicators" from which to choose. One you may find helpful, as demonstrated on the Endeavour Silver chart, is the moving average convergent divergent (MACD) signal, which helps show important price turns, along with the momentum driving them. Ideally, if a stock is dropping sharply, the MACD should do so as well. (If not, the ensuing signal is called a "non-confirmation."

A big TA tool informing your trading is the Moving Average. These run anywhere from a few days to years. The two most commonly followed are the 50 Day and the 200 Day Moving Average (DMA). A stock is deemed to be in a solid uptrend when the 50 Day is above the 200 Day and both are rising. Turn this statement around, and you have a downtrend. A 50 Day crossing over the 200 Day to the downside is sometimes called a "Death Cross", indicating the possibility of a trend reversal of intermediate to long term duration. You should be aware, however, that "whipsaws" occur with this indicator.

**A valuable moving average trade tactic, is to watch for a stock or group of stocks that have become extended from their 50 Day MA. In a robust bull market, a reaction will cause a temporarily decline into the area of the 50 Day line. Before the uptrend resumes, it may be possible to add to your position just above or below this line. A deeper correction, as exemplified by the one which took place in late 2016, will drive down toward the 200 DMA.

A technical tutorial

An example demonstrating this concept took place in late August, 2016. After an epic multiple-month run to the upside, a serious - and necessary - correction finally got underway. Mining share prices broke sharply across the board. For the investor looking to either purchase more shares or set up core positions <u>and who believed that the bull trend was still intact,</u> an excellent approach would have been to place first tranche Limit Buy orders around a given stock's 50 day Moving Average, with a second tranche deeper, and a third order around the 200 day MA. This kind of behavior goes against the grain, but it's exactly what must be done in order to capture big profits. If and as prices dip into these lower zones, expect to hear a host of bearish comments, making following through with your program even more difficult.

Stu Thomson addresses the emotional tides with which all traders must contend:

> **"We're _all_ cowards on price weakness. Those who admit it, those who bet against it make money. Those who hide it and lie about it, lose money. End of story."**

First, Observe: Do the fundamental and technical drivers (major technical HSR in support of the sector's bullish thesis, etc.) still appear to be valid?

Second, Orient: Does this fit your strategic picture of establishing/ adding to a core position into great weakness?

Third, Decide: Have you built a short list of "best of breed" stocks you believe will be powerful movers to the upside once the correction has run its course? Have you done the math on available funds so you can buy in a way that does not overweight a given stock, and which reserves financial firepower to add more if prices drop well below what you expect?

For illustration purposes only -we could have chosen dozens more that had this same formation - look at the First Majestic waterfall decline in August-September, 2016. A strategy for the committed bullish trader might have been to establish three limit buy tranches: First around the 50 Day MA at $15.05 (avoiding round numbers); Second at $11.05 - representing a 50% retracement of the entire year's up move); the Third at

$7.22 - representing, <u>on the weekly chart</u>, the rising 50 Day MA and the critical breakout area above the 2015 highs.

Assuming the secular bull trend was still alive, this lower area should present massive HSR (Horizontal Support - to catch/support prices, with resistance to dropping prices). Be aware that you might not achieve all of these fills. What is important is that you have once again made a plan, following the four steps we've discussed - including that last critical action - your plan's execution. Over time you will become more accomplished... and most likely grow your account balance in tandem.

OODA Loop Execution Model Example

Fourth, Act!: After the first three steps, are you still a believer in your own planning? Will you have the courage to act? Here's what the late Sir John Templeton, an investment giant had to say about this:

> "We humans are instinctively herd animals, and we
> tend to panic when we see others around us panicking.
> We lose our independent judgment and we freeze in fear
> at exactly the moment we should be buying aggressively."

And Jim Sinclair ("Mr. Gold"), the largest gold futures trader in the 1980 gold bull market:

"How do you make really big money in the market?
You have to identify your point of <u>maximum pain</u>. That's
the point where you really want to go into the bathroom
and slit your wrists. Identify that exact point, and then…
you must buy."

The longer term MAs are deemed to offer either greater confirmation
of a major trend change, or the continuation of one. For the purpose of
discussion, in mid-2016, analysts noted that the performance ratio of gold
to gold stocks (as measured by indices, had after 20 years, turned in favor
of gold stocks. (shortly after the breakout, the ratio went vertical. Should
this new trend continue to develop, it would indicate that in relative
terms, gold stocks are in the process of re-establishing their tendency to
outperform the gold price.

Indeed this is expected by mining stock traders, because gold stocks
are inherently more risky than holding the metal itself. A 2-3x miner
outperformance serves as justification for even participating in the sector
as opposed to simply holding physical gold (thereby dealing with only a
single risk factor - the price decline of the metal itself - vs. a host of "risk
issues" with a given miner. This could be very good news for those who
trade mining stocks, because it would be an early indicator of a lengthy
period of miner <u>outperformance</u>, on top of a robust increase in the price
of gold itself. Icing on the profits cake.

There's a caveat about the use of TA. We know of several newsletter
writers who have become so "involved" with trying to interpret and evaluate
all the squiggles and "indicators" (some Elliott Wavers, are you listening?),
that at important market turns, they have a tendency to mentally "lock
up" and try to pressure the market into doing what they expect. This
happened to a couple of well-known analysts in 2000 (who had earlier
achieved prominence going into the 1980 commodities top), when instead
of buying gold at around $275, they kept waiting because their brand of
TA "proved" it would drop to $180 first. But Mr. Market was not aware
of this expectation, and during 11 consecutive years of higher prices, gold
managed to rise instead by over 600%.

When investors were staring into the abyss late in 2015, a chorus of TA
types just "knew" that gold would drop to $950, or even $700 and silver

to $10, where they would advise their acolytes to "back up the truck" and get long. These folks tended to define themselves as "long term bullish, short term bearish". We think a fair number of investors who diligently followed these pied pipers are still waiting with their portfolio trucks on idle... and empty. What seems increasingly likely is that these "short-term bears" are going to end up "long-term empty handed."

When the market occasionally starts acting "out of character"-not accommodating the analyst's preferences - the Luke Skywalker *Star Wars* analogy has a certain resonance. In the heat of battle, having been tasked with destroying the Death Star and seeing his wingmen being shot down around him, Luke listened to the spirit of *Obe Wan Kenobe* telling him, "Luke, just turn off your computer!" He did so without anticipation, letting his skill and equipment blend with circumstances in the moment. Since he could no longer be tracked, he was able to survive the approach, hone in on the planet-sized weapons field's vulnerable core and destroy it.

We posit that the day will come, when in order to survive with ones financial hide intact against what the future may have in store for us, you - and we - will have to do the same.

TA Conclusions and a Look Ahead...

It's safe to say that most investors pay a fair amount of attention to charts. At least they tell you where prices have been. Often, they provide a warning as to whether the price is "too high" or "too low" so that decisions can be made accordingly.

At the intermediate high point in silver in May, 2011, David Morgan called the top within one day, and this writer (David Smith) called it a day after that. DM can prove it via archival data he shared at the time with subscribers to *The Morgan Report*. This writer did so in an email to mining stock Analyst, writer, and bullion sales dealer, Greg McCoach.

Ok, maybe we were just lucky. But the fact remains, that paying attention to the charts, listening to market sentiment, looking at technical indicators like the 50 day and 200 day MAs, as well as assorted chart patterns, and the bullish consensus, enabled us to make our calls with a fair degree of confidence. Certainly, when they were placed within the context of a subjective risk/reward scenario, underlain with years of experience.

Does anyone including us, always get it right? Of course not. But once in awhile when all the ducks line up - including listening to our gut - we hit the sweet spot and "nail it". People have been known to say that charting is just voodoo analysis. They could have a point, because sometimes several people can look at the same chart and come away with completely different opinions. But the fact remains that the majority of market participants follow charts and attempt to interpret them via technical analysis. And while we would be among the first to admit that charts can lead their users astray, it would be foolish of us - and you - to ignore the value of the important things they may be able to tell us.

The Day will come when *The Morgan Report* will attempt to call the ultimate precious metals bull market top.

One of the things David Morgan has long told subscribers, is that he intends to apply all his skills, in order to alert readers so they have an opportunity to get out at a point near the secular bull market's top. It will be both his call <u>and</u> theirs. This could enable those who choose to take his recommendation, to leave the party while most other investors and speculators are still "celebrating". Increasing the odds he'll be able to pull this feat off, will be his reliance on several decades of market participation, his understanding of investor sentiment (as well as his own), intuition, and yes, a serious study of the charts.

Note: We are aware of many in the precious metals community who make fun of, or plainly state that TA does not work! Unfortunately they may never have studied technical analysis, nor understand that the basis for the high frequency trading they often talk about is predicated entirely upon—you guessed it - technical analysis. Further, ALL major broker-dealers use TA in their decision-making. Is it a perfect science? No. However, to neglect it out of hand based upon an unexamined bias, when nothing can show manipulation better than technical analysis leaves us baffled.

The market tends to give us the price first and the reasons later. So it's reasonable to expect that <u>fundamental</u> changes big enough to upend what we believe will be an upside run for the history books, will make themselves known well after the ultimate price points have been printed.

Third: Institute and Follow sound Money Management 101 practices

Decide how much to commit to your campaign beforehand. Use stop losses - preferably mental, so you're not picked off by the market makers. Seldom add to a "losing" position (except when buying in tranches – see later), and take profits from time to time, perhaps when you've scored a double -see discussion below.

Sell and buy trading satellites; Hold the Core... and know the difference!

The initial 2016 upstream launch from depressed levels that prevailed during the preceding several years, in many cases plumbing historic lows, ran for a number of months with only a few short, sometimes violent corrections lasting a few days, to less than a few weeks. Many stocks gave back no more than 20% of their best print before taking off again and establishing another new high. Looking at the situation late into 2016, we can make some pertinent observations about our thesis - one of which is critical. Reflect upon this if your goal is to achieve a 10x yield <u>and</u> still be a player into the mania phase for some potentially "yuuge" gains which could become available at that time.

Build a core of what you feel are the "best and brightest" mining stocks, plus a streamer or two, and maybe a "prospect generator." Your choice of "names" may be as few as 10 or 12. They should keep on giving to your bottom line as long as the primary trend is up. If a company blows up, gets nationalized, or starts underperforming on an intermediate basis, "fire it" and find a better story, or add to one that is rewarding you, but to which you may have only committed a small percentage of funds. Use ETFs primarily as trading vehicles.

This is where making a distinction between "core" and "trading" holdings - and sticking with it - becomes an important part of the discussion. There are traders who can sell half their position into a strong rise, place a new order 25% lower, get filled and end up with an even larger holding of a given stock... accomplishing a lower breakeven price to boot. This is all well and good. But if you miss on this kind of trade, and rather than jumping back in, watch for a week or two, are you willing to buy back the stock you sold at $6.50, again at $10? Or watch it rise even further for a number of months before re-buying? The reality is that most people hesitate, and in the event will not act.

Therefore, you MUST hold the Core until you believe the primary secular trend is rolling over, or until you think - based upon some level of research - that a major cyclical bear, counter to the primary trend is underway. This absolutely critical distinction has to be made, if you intend to maximize profits on the way to the ultimate high print for this major bull market cycle.

"Taking a Free Ride" with Discretion.

A lot of people "make money" in the markets, but relatively few "keep it", because they never sell anything. It's the theme of Bob Moriarty's book, *Nobody Knows Anything*. It's a concept commented on by the best analysts. It's a *leitmotif* of the book you are now reading. Taking a profit occasionally provides essential nourishment for the trader's soul, reinforces the correctness of his/her trading campaign, and keeps some earnings from the swings of one of the most volatile investments on the planet - mining stocks. With good reason, Doug Casey has called them "burning matches." Where else can you find dozens of stocks that can rise 1000%, decline 95%, then do it again? Or somewhere on this roller coaster continuum, drop 100% and be delisted into the Gray Market, trading for fractions of a penny per share... if at all? Welcome to the world of resource sector stocks!

Selling one-half your position on a double has a lot to recommend it. Popularly known as the "Casey Free Ride" after Doug Casey - this idea was first proposed by Marin Katusa, so that's how we'll refer to it - the "Katusa Free Ride" (KFR).

In this situation, when your position has earned a 100% profit, you might sell one-half, taking out what was invested for your original stake. Of course you will have to decide what works best for you, but given the vibrancy thus far of the initial up leg since January, 2016, and the short, shallow corrections it has evidenced as of this writing, it makes sense to modify Marin's rule when it comes to paring down your positions into heavy strength. This would be especially true for those who started their positions in December 2015.

If, after your first double, you had been quick to take a Katusa Free

Ride on half your position, you would have found yourself with a much smaller number of shares in your mining stock portfolio in July than when you started in January. Why? Because during most of 2016, many of the quality stocks, and even a lot of the dogs, doubled, tripled or quadrupled from their bear market lows. You could choose by throwing darts and be up 150%. So, if you sold half each time you got a double... and IF you were *not* able to reposition into the relatively brief retracements preparatory to another run to the upside, then after 6 months or so, you probably had (have?) as little as 10 - 20% of the position size with which you began the year.

We posit that if you intend to achieve 10x or more portfolio growth during this cycle, you're going to have to leave "well enough alone" - at certain times - and with certain elements of your stock position. This will mean delineating quite clearly - for you - what constitutes the unassailable inner core you will rarely touch until the secular move seems to be over. The "outer core" or speculative positions are the ones where you will be looking to take the free ride trades.

Ours sense is that application of the Katusa Free Ride is at its most beneficial in two specific circumstances. First, when dealing with a position you hold in a highly-speculative exploration play that is moving through an extremely volatile "price discovery" phase. The price might shoot up 5x on a big announcement; drop back 3x awaiting further news; then jump another 6x on the next leg up, etc. On that first big move, by taking the KFR, you would now be "debt free", with your original investment money back in your account - thereafter playing solely with "the house money".

Think BIG. Win BIG.

The second best time for the KFR would be during a broad sideways consolidation period in the sector itself, when prices are bouncing between two widely-spaced horizontal support-resistance (HSR) chart rails. This situation can last for several weeks or even months, during which time your offsets will be providing "profit vitamins", lowering your cost basis, while rebuilding your speculative position within the obvious chart boundaries that other traders are also watching - and acting upon, day by day.

This issue will come up again near the end of the bull market, when automatically selling at a 100% profit may cost you - within a short time - another 300% on that stock! For the most part, "just say no" to selling Core positions. Create most of the action using your satellite holdings.

If you took one or more "free rides" in 2016, take a look at two silver stocks we noticed out of several dozen, which demonstrate not only this point, but also hint at the longer-term price appreciation that you could end up missing.

Silver mining stock "A": 2015 Bear market low -$0.09 cents; July 1, 2016 close: US$ 0.64 cents; % rise, 722%. If you had sold half your position after each double, even assuming you got back in with more shares at say a 20% discount half the time - a major assumption unless you remained glued to a real-time quote screen, it's a safe bet that you now would have only a fraction of your original substantial position. Now consider that **the 2011 high for this miner was $3.20.**

Silver mining stock "B": 2015 Bear market low - USD$0.22 cents; July 1, 2016 close: US$1.93; % rise: 875%. See previous paragraph describing mining stock "A", beginning with "If you had sold half your position after each double, you would have..." Oh, and by the way, **the 2011 high for this miner was $10.28.**

Our unscientific take about this, based upon having read almost all of the publicly-disseminated analysts' recommendations and a fair amount of opinions given specifically to subscribers during the year, (we too subscribe to a number of other letters in the sector) is that a great many investors missed 40-60% of the 2016 upside explosion. A number of analysts, some having written about this sector for 10-15 years, had their readers out of the market during much of the first seven months. This was to become one of the biggest, fastest rising sectors from historically depressed levels ever. Jim Flanagan probably does as much "way back" research on bull and bear legs, comparing them to present day conditions for trading ideas, as anyone else in the business. During the last week of July, 2016, he made the following statement:

> "The 175% Advance in Gold Stocks in 5 Months, 22 Days Now Places Us As the 11th Greatest 1st Leg Up in Any Bull Market in Any of the Tangible Assets During the Past 150 Years. In Other Words, it is the Elite of the Elite."

It's likely that legions of gold and silver bug wannabes, who, while waiting from a 100% cash position and bated breath for $950 gold and $10 silver, missed the whole run! Or, who were simply too shell-shocked and disbelieving after the previous 5 year grind to force themselves to act. Stu Thomson at Graceland Updates nailed it - "If you trade looking through a microscope, your profits will be... microscopic!"

One important caveat: (Not to add confusion to the above, but think this one through and see if you agree) - During what you have come to feel are the later stages of an extended run such as we witnessed into early September, 2016 - it is entirely appropriate - and necessary - to start selling your underperformers, some of the "moon shot" holdings and even some shares of a core position which has become too large within the context of your total dollar holdings. This is going to help you raise money to add to/re-buy shares lower with the expected intermediate correction gets fully underway. As we are writing this, the metals and miners are undergoing a severe correction, in some cases retracing 50% or more of a given stocks 2016 rise. By placing tranches of Limit Buy/GTC orders within the broad belt of 50 and 200 Day Moving Averages, some excellent fills can take place. Indeed two of our core holdings were filled around the 200 DMA this way... at 55% off their best price print earlier in the summer!

What to expect for gold into 2017 and beyond.

The bear market we've just experienced ran from 2011 (May for silver, Sept for gold), until late 2015-early 2016. This ferocious and protracted counter-trend to the secular cycle cut almost 45% off the gold price, 70% for silver, and 70 - 99% (or more for many hapless companies that simply dried up and blew away!) of value from mining companies' share prices. Depending upon what metric you follow, this protracted blood-bath was arguably the worst (deepest) of the last 60-90 years.

No one who is honest with you - including us - claims to have foreseen the duration and depth into which this sector fell. HOWEVER, if you look at the table listing the last several gold bear markets, an interesting statistic comes into view. In the last downturn, which presumably ended in December, 2015, gold fell about 44% from its 2011 high - in line with previous major gold declines averaging the same 44%. (Silver declined considerably more, which was to be expected, due to its greater volatility.)

Table 2: Gold has experienced five bear and bull cycles since the 1970s*					
Bull market			Bear market		
Dates	M	Cumulative return	Dates	M	Cumulative return
1/70-1/75	61	451.4%	1/75-9/76	20	-46.4%
10/76-2/80	41	721.3%	2/80-3/85	61	-55.9%
3/85-12/87	33	75.8%	12/87-3/93	63	-34.7%
4/93-2/96	35	27.2%	2/96-9/99	43	-39.1%
10/99-9/11	144	649.6%	9/11-12/15	52	-44.1%
Average	63	385.1%	Average†	47	-44.0%
Median	41	451.4%	Median†	52	-42.7%

*We are defining a bull market as a period where US dollar gold prices rose for at least two consecutive years and bear markets as the subsequent periods where the price generally fell for a sustained time.

M=length in months.

†Excludes the period from September 2011 to December 2015.

Source: Bloomberg, ICE Benchmark Administration Ltd, World Gold Council

Gold Bull and Bear Cycles
Courtesy Sources Listed

A deep dive into this gold bull/bear cycle table brings up an interesting proposition - one especially germane to our premise that the profit opportunity going forward for gold/silver/the mining shares should be considerably larger than a cursory look at even this table would suggest. It's because these statistics do not distinguish between a cyclical gold rise during a major secular bear market like the one between 1980 and 2000, as related to what the yellow metal does during a full-fledged secular bull run.

In a secular bear, you have occasional major cyclical bull runs that remain within the context and confines of the larger, longer bearish secular range. Every one of them is destined to fail, dropping eventually down into the final secular low. Depending upon the elements present as the bear is breathing its last, the bottom may be either a spike low, a grinding "sandpaper" finale, or a long drawn out sideways price action that bores everyone to death, so that all but the most diehard participants give up in disgust. Which is exactly where the investment greats like Sir John Templeton and Jim Rogers would be "heading over to the corner to pick up the money." During the current mining cycle, some of those active names would be Pierre Lassonde, Rick Rule, Ross Beaty, Dr. Keith Barron, Bob Quartermain, Doug Casey, and the like.

Thus, it can be argued that the two advance and decline cycles shown, taking place as they did between 1985 - 1999, should be seen within this context, from the 1980 major gold-silver top until roughly 2000-01, when the metals and miners finally put in their long-term bottom. Delete those two cyclical up-turns, and you have <u>an average secular bull market profit potential of over 600%</u>. If history comes even close to repeating itself, the likelihood of some very serious profits in this sector is a situation we're facing dead ahead!

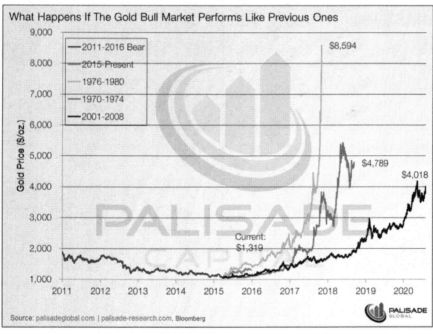

Comparative Gold Bull Markets (Courtesy Palisade Global)

Riding the Wave: Making sure you're standing for the "last eighth".

In late 2015, Rick Rule spoke about Eric Sprott, saying "Eric has always said, 'Don't be afraid to be right'. That's where we are right now... This is the time when the 'A' players go to war."

And, "If you believe you're right and the data says hold your ground—you hold your ground. Normally there's a pretty big payday at the end."

All secular bull markets go through one - sometimes several - severe declines on their way to the final, lasting top. Take any market you want, from soybeans and sugar to the 2000 Tech Wreck... to silver and gold in 1980. It's generally agreed upon that these markets will experience three major up legs. Furthermore - as laid out about precious metals during the last few years by David Morgan in his writings and conference presentations - the third and last leg offers the potential for as much as 80-90% of the bull's profit potential... which becomes available during the last 10% in time of the entire progression!

A premise in this book is that it's highly probable the spot gold and silver price levels posted during the December time-frame, along with the final mining stock washout in mid-January 2016, represented the culmination of the multi-year cyclical bear market which began in mid-late 2011. If so, we are looking at the initial stages of the third and greatest secular bull market leg, which began during the 1998-2004 period. Yes, we'll see more "retracements". Most will be relatively short and violent in nature. They will last from just a few days during a runaway phase, to a couple of weeks during a "garden variety" correction; and from time to time, a retracement of several months. But as such, prior to the ultimate secular top we do not anticipate another cyclical metals' bear market that's anything near the scale, depth, and duration of the 2011-15 debacle.

Our view about how far out the Big Top is, and in what price range it's likely to take place is subject to refinement as time passes and new inputs come into play. It could be 2-3 years from now. Or it might be 5-7 years away. But we'll say this - You should be paying a lot of attention to the first quarter of each of these years: 2018, 2019, 2020, and 2022. When the ultimate price is finally printed, the odds are very good that it will take place during the first half of the year; highly probable that it will be by April of a given year; and in our view, <u>extremely likely</u> that it will be in either January or February of a given year.

To Summarize: The components of designing and executing a successful investment plan are - cultivating the Mind by constantly cycling through The OODA Loop; learning about, implementing Fundamental and Technical analysis; and following sound money management tactics. These salutary behaviors will do wonders for keeping your investment boat afloat, high in the water, and capable of carrying you safely to the far shore, laden with sustained and increasingly-larger profits.

Constantly sharpen your understanding and implementation of <u>all three</u> of these concepts. Each "leg" is so important, that as Dr. Alexander Elder remarks, "Remove one, and the stool will fall, together with the person who sits on it."

If you can achieve even a basic proficiency in doing these things, you're likely to be around for that "last eighth." If you think you've seen some exciting price action so far, well, my friend... You ain't seen nothing yet!

The Tao of Using Stops to get in and out of a position

It's generally better to keep stop losses "mental," with activation on a close of day basis, rather than formally placing them in the market with your broker. If your stop is at an obvious price-point on the charts, you may be "picked off" intraday on an engineered price plunge, only to have the market reverse/close higher.

If you do choose to place formal stop losses, there are a couple of ways to go about it. Once you've taken a position and determined where you'd like to get out if the market disagrees with your opinion, place an order either termed **"Stop-Market"** - a price which becomes a Market Order when touched, or **"Stop-Limit"** - a price which when activated, will only be filled at that amount or better. Keep in mind that in a highly volatile situation, either procedure can cause unintended consequences. In the case of a Stop-Market, a sharp drop may give you a fill somewhat or substantially lower than your activation price. For a Stop-Limit, a quickly-dropping market may bypass your limit order, and if prices to not rise again to touch it, you may not get a fill at all. (Use this terminology also to work orders above the current market price.)

Here's an unsettling example. Management of a $6.00 mining stock announces their property has been nationalized by the host government. The stock opens at $5, your stop-market is at $4.50, and it gets filled at $3.90 as the market for that stock collapses. Another investor also had his stop at $4.50, but it was a "stop-limit." Prices quickly fell through his price, spent an hour trading just below $4.00, then closed on the day at $1.50.

But the $4.50 stop-limit price was never filled and our hapless investor still holds his position, now worth $1.50 per share. You've just witnessed an example of the old adage that he who loses least, wins...

You can subscribe to a commercially available stop-loss service that adjusts your stops so they "trail" an ascending market price. The intent is to keep you in the position as long as possible, while holding onto a certain pre-determined profit, should the market make a substantial turn (by the percentage chosen) against your position.

We know of one major limited-service brokerage house in particular offering this service without charge to its clients who have a certain account balance. (Check around, there may be others.) They provide what's called **"T-Stop%"** and **"T-Stop $"**. The former auto-adjusts your predetermined % away from the market's price. as a trailing stop-loss. The latter adjusts it within a specific dollar amount upon which you've previously decided.

Generally speaking, your formally-entered stop-loss should be listed as "Good 'til Cancelled" (GTC). This will usually be in effect for 60 - 90 days (Be sure to confirm your broker's policies.). If you're trading a stock on a major exchange, you may be able to use a stop called "GTC + Extended Hours". Having a window before and after the normal day's session may come in handy if adverse - or beneficial - news strikes before the next day's formal session, enabling you to act before the full force of the crowd crashes against your position.

Keep a Cash Reserve

Only in very rare, very special and well-thought out circumstances, should you be without a cash reserve. It may be 5-20%, but keep some cash on hand. Holding cash serves a psychological function. You know that you could take another position if you wanted. It's like giving yourself permission to have that bottle of cola. Go without acting on your "permission" for awhile, and before long, you'll have little desire to trade without a sound reason. Over time, this habit helps dampen the tendency to overtrade.

Don't expect to sell a position and immediately be able to buy something else. If you frequently trade Canadian mining stocks, you may have to wait 3 market days for the cash received from a sale to clear. This could short-circuit your plans to do a fast sell and re-buy.

Position Sizing

Something to be careful of is becoming enamored with a particular stock "story" to the point you plunge into a position so large in relation to your total account funds, that you become vulnerable to an untoward event - be it an act of nature, man - or both.

- A tailings' dam breaks, flooding the surrounding countryside, causing an uproar internationally, and operations are closed down indefinitely.
- $5 billion dollars is spent on a "world-class" gold and silver deposit, when questions about legal ownership, and environmental concerns place the entire project into developmental limbo for many years.
- One of the largest gold finds in the last 30 years is nationalized by the host government, wiping out management and shareholder equity.
- An "x" times 100 moz silver deposit is removed by court decree from the ownership of one company and awarded to another. The next day, the shares of Company 'A' decline 90%; those of Company 'B' surge by 10x.
- Tens of millions of dollars are spent on (two separate companies' projects - one for gold, one silver). Nearing production, further geological work indicates that most of the ounces which were believed to exist on the property are no more than wishful thinking. Both companies go bankrupt.
- An exploration company in South America spends $32 million infill drilling and building infrastructure on a very rich silver

property. Metals prices go into an unprecedented multiple-year decline, the company loses the project, and sells out their operations for $800,000.

- A silver mining company in the U.S. whose shares once traded for over $40 apiece, confronts the need to spend $1 billion dollars to expand production, fails to raise a fraction of that amount during tough economic times... and goes to $0.00 per share.

These examples are all taken from the annals of actual resource sector mining and exploration events during the last decade. We could have listed quite a few more. Sure, you might have been "overweight" in one of the big-deal success stories that returned 20 or 50x to shareholders, rather than what happened here.

But if you spread out the risk a bit, and avoid going "all-in" on ANY project, regardless of how incredibly amazing it looks, you will be able to survive a number of financial hits to companies that underperform, get nationalized or blow up... and still be around to make serious money and sit at the Winners' Table when this whole story has played itself out. The next time you feel like placing all of your chips on one or two companies, imagine yourself looking down the barrel of Dirty Harry's .44 magnum revolver, because that's just what Mr. Market will be pointing at you. He may be smiling at the time, but the riddle will be the same - "Well, punk, do you feel lucky today?"

Buying in tranches is <u>not</u> the same as "averaging down"

The idea of buying in portions or tranches into weakness is totally different from the questionable practice of "averaging down"! When averaging down, a person places a bet on a particular investment, expecting (of course!) that it will rise in price. If it doesn't, and begins to fall, the investor is faced with a loss. Rather than sell out, he/she hopes the price will rise, and so out of fear, buys more.

The belief is that if the price rises enough, the position will get back to "break even", so it can be sold without a loss. But too often the price keeps falling. Also too often, the investor continues to average down, buying more. At some point, he panics and sells the entire position for a big loss, most likely right at the bottom. Simply stated: averaging down on the same stock (investment) can wipe you out!

Lest you think this happens only to small fish, consider that in 2011, the wealthiest man in Ireland declared bankruptcy. Listed by Forbes as worth $6 billion and as the 164th richest man in the world, he bought leveraged CDFs ("contracts for difference") on an Irish bank. As its shares declined, he was encouraged to borrow hundreds of millions of dollars and buy more shares. When he could no longer meet margin calls, he went down. He had made two mistakes - Using leverage and staking everything on one position. Be very leery of attempting to go head to head with Mr. Market!

Of all the trading techniques this writer (David Smith) has tried over the years, the idea of buying *tranches* into weakness with a pre-determined amount of money, buying "smaller than is rational" - and deciding beforehand how much you will commit to that particular idea - has done more than any other behavior to reduce the market's emotional impact on his thinking and trading. Fear is reduced. Greed is reduced. You're more relaxed when the markets are open, and after the day's session. With today's market volatility, computer-generated High Frequency Trading can cause a "flash crash" within a matter of minutes and just as quickly recover. Keeping calm is a critical skill to master. Doing so can and will give you an enormously powerful investment edge. And it just might keep you from blowing up your account before you can corral the financial largess for which you so ardently strive.

Three Important Trading Behavior Traits

1. As your account balance grows, do not keep allocating the same percentage to a given idea (stock) that you did when it was smaller. In the early days when you had a $40,000 dollar account balance, you might have felt the need to devote 5 or even 10% to a trade in order to grow your balance quickly. If that questionable money management practice worked out, then you may have grown your balance substantially. But if you keep doing this, when your account may now be $300,000, sooner or later, after a series of trading mistakes, you will likely blow yourself out of the water. For example, you might

have used $4,000 (10% of your account balance) on a trade. But now, rather than devoting the same percentage of your larger holdings, continue to use $4,000 as opposed to $30,000. Do you see how you are now risking <u>much</u> less money per trade, AND are less likely to encounter the concept of "the probability of ruin"? You will more likely survive and later prosper, should Mr. Market unexpectedly decide to take you for a wild ride, before letting you get back in step with your earlier profitable ways.

2. Let's say you have "a dog that won't hunt", or you've tried, as Louis James likes to say "to catch a falling safe before it hits the ground". After serious reflection, if you've decided that stock is unlikely to revive soon, if ever, sell it! Even if you only get pennies on the dollar, <u>immediately</u> place those funds into a stock which your research has demonstrated has excellent growth potential. The psychological lift of doing this is not to be underestimated, because having acted upon getting rid of that loser, your mind will be free, closure will have been accomplished, and your full abilities now available to manage the rest of your positions.

3. If you determine you've made an offset mistake - don't keep making it! Let's say you sold x shares of a gold miner that was "overbought", for $8.00. During the coming days it continued to rise, making new highs into $8.60. You ask yourself why you ever sold it, and cannot find a good answer. Don't be afraid to buy it back, therefore paying more than when you offset the position. If it is a good stock, it may run to $12.00, while you watch! Will you buy it back at $12? Probably not.

To Summarize:

Stewart Thomson, to whom I (David Smith) owe an enormous debt of gratitude for the trading acumen he has helped me to develop over the years through his writing, puts it in his mentoring-investment letter, *Graceland Updates,* this way:

> "It's a long process. No champion is built by opening
> up a crackerjack box and pulling out a U.S. debt clock prize
> that says 'free gold parabola for you!' Wealth-building is

a mindset. It's a mindset that takes years to build. (But) Once built, it's unbreakable....

"It's very important for the gambler who sells, not to try to "get back in" right away or even for a long time. Wait for all the greed to disappear. Wait for the horror and the agony to appear. Wait until you don't just think price is going far lower, but wait until you KNOW that. Then bet against what you supposedly know, eat a mountain of pain, and buy, with size that is smaller than you know is rational. Then, the professional gambler will start getting richer, consistently."

Takeaways:

- Respond to (buy/sell), rather than try and predict market movement.
- Invert your emotions: Buy a bit into Weakness; Sell a bit into Strength.
- Understand the effect of High Frequency Trading (HFT) on metals' prices.
- Expect Volatility (40-50% swings for Producers; 60-80% for Explorers).
- Keep your picture "Big"!
- Make The OODA Loop your default operating platform.
- Practice The Pareto Principle (20% of the effort yields 80% of the results.)
- Conserve and build your "Psychological Capital".
- Keep aligned with the primary trend.
- Mining shares come into their own late in the bull market cycle - starting now!
- ALL Investors (including the Chinese!) are price chasers.

CHAPTER 5

A TEN TIMES Your Money Precious Metals' Battle Plan: Part I

> *Only you can determine for yourself how you want to play this new bull market in the precious metals stocks. For some it will be a life changing event, and for others it will be a should of or could of kind of bull market.* - **Rambus**

For investors/speculators who by accident or design end up remaining in the market well into the topping process of the continuing precious metals' bull run, achieving a profit of ten times (1,000%) or more on *several* quality mining stocks in their portfolio is entirely possible. Holding story stocks too long represents a high degree of risk. Common wisdom states that the extra volatility of mining stocks over the precious metals themselves, is more than made up for the fact that they tend to rise at least three times as much as the underlying metal. Until early 2016, the mining equities *underperformed* the metal, which means that if or when the physical demand overwhelms the market, these shares may go even further than expected

Several reasons accounted for this performance disparity. In the 1970's bull run, there were less "parallel mining investment vehicles" available to drain off speculation dollars into other venues. For example, take Exchange Traded Funds (ETFs). Even though ETFs began trading in the 1980's, they didn't really accelerate in terms of availability, multiplicity of choice, and investment popularity until 2005. There are now almost 5,000 (as a category, more correctly referred to as *exchange-traded products* - ETPs).

In the mining/metals' sector, we now have ETFs like the Silver Miners SIL, with a basket of silver producers; GDXJ, which holds gold and silver exploration companies/early-stage producers - and the list goes on. So a potential flood of money that might have gone directly into the shares of producers and exploration plays of all stripes - yielding over-performance in relation to the rise in price of the metals they produce, was instead diffused into a plethora of ETPs.

Another factor, apparent since the 2011 downturn, but actually having its genesis with the 2008 financial collapse that spread across almost all asset categories, has been the massive commodities bust. This state of affairs can be seen, later in this chapter, with the chart of the TSX-V, the Canadian exchange where a large share of the world's resource sector companies are traded.

In retrospect, the move up by the index back into mid-2011 was simply a classic 2/3rds retracement of the bull market move that had played itself out during the late 2002 - early 2009 period. Its failure thereafter gave fair warning that the mining stocks were in serious trouble and had yet to find a bottom. (This disparity is also amply demonstrated when looking at the Baltic Dry Index (BDI) - a measure of goods' shipping activity around the globe.) And what a bottom the November, 2015 - January 19, 2016 foundational low turned out to be!

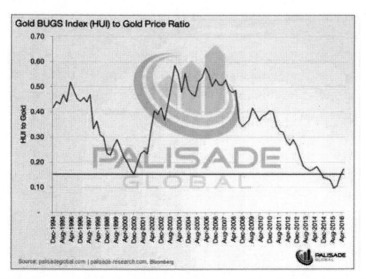

Gold Bugs Index - Gold Price Ratio (courtesy Palisade Global)

HUI vs. Gold Price (miners massively underperforming) - so far...

It was only slightly higher than in 1999, yet in many ways, actually worse. Hundreds of TSX resource sector companies were delisted; hundreds more turned into "zombies" - lacking money to do more than file financial statements and perform share roll-backs of twenty or fifty to one; in some cases, one hundred to one roll backs. A few literally went to pot, promoting the green weed instead of searching for green-field exploration opportunities.

Even those who survived often saw their price drop over 90% from the mid- 2011 highs. Two unnamed examples of silver producers should suffice to bear this out. Silver producer company "A" - 2011 high: $26.80 per share... January 2016 low: $2.40. Company "B" - 2011 high: $13.00... 2015 Low: $1.00. These two companies are primary silver producers with robust properties, and excellent management. As metals' prices fell, they survived by cutting expenses and constantly lowered all-in-sustaining-costs (AISC) - one of the most reliable indicators of a mining company's per ounce profitability - or lack thereof.

Another factor contributing to the underperformance of the miners was the flood of new share issuance many companies pumped into the market during the decade-long run up into the 2011 price peak. These paper share placements added deleterious effects to a sector already burdened by falling prices. When good money goes into bad companies and is lost, it means less funding for other more viable selections.

However, the better quality mining stocks now appear capable of reasserting their vaunted outperformance as a sector for the rest of the evolving bull run. We think the next bull move could continue for another 3 - 5 years... perhaps longer. From the world's largest gold miner, Barrick Gold, to many of the "juniors", the survivors, over last few years of downturn have made it a priority to reduce production, administrative and exploration costs. Then, if need be, shed properties that could only become economically-viable at much higher metals' prices. In short, leaner, meaner producers - to an investor's benefit - are now over-represented in the sector.

With the rise in 2016 Q1-3 share prices, most of these stalwarts are up substantially on a percentage basis from their Year to Date (YTD) lows.

However, when you see a stock that has run from $0.95 cents to $3.50, and that very same stock sold for $15.00 in 2011, when it was producing 30% less silver then than it does now, it's not pie-in-the sky to feel that there's a lot of "upside" as metals move to challenge their 2011 nominal dollar highs... and beyond.

Supportive of this premise, keep the following in mind. From the 2011 Top to bottom at the end of December 2015, the mining stocks' indices declined a whopping 88%. This means the stock you might have been able to buy at the beginning of 2016, intraday, for $0.22 cents, could be trading at $2 or more/share now.

Yet in 2011, that very same stock - with just one mine where it now has two - sold for $10.20. Just getting back to those highs still gives you almost a 5-bagger from here, without the precious metals going beyond their own previous highs. Are gold and silver prices destined to break out above their $1,900 + and $50 respective highs? We believe they are, on the way to the public mania blow-off which looks to be a near- certainty within the next few years. If so, you might see another digit added to some of these "10-bagger" candidates!

The 1980 top shows that mining stocks as a group continued to advance for <u>some time after the metals did</u> before topping out. So not only is the upside likely to be working in your favor, but if this pattern is repeated, so is the time extension for allowing the better mining stocks to achieve their best potential.

A Word about Risk.

In today's marketplace, virtually any investment you make is going to be associated with risk. Even choosing <u>not</u> to invest is risky! Keep your money under a mattress? Inflation risk. Hold it in a savings account? The paltry interest accrued, well below the inflation rate, means your purchasing power is eaten steadily by inflation, while you're taxed on the illusory "interest" the bank decides to pay. Not to mention a possible "bail in" where your money is used to keep the bank solvent. If and when negative interest rates (NIRP) come to your bank, you will be *penalized* for keeping a balance! Imagine paying the bank for the privilege of having money in your own account!

In parts of Europe, this is already a fact of life. Adding insult to injury, a bank (as was done in Spain during the last downturn) might force conversion of your balance into bank shares. In the aforementioned Spanish case, the bank's shares promptly lost 90% of their value... with a similar effect on their customers' forced account conversions.

So forget about avoiding risk. But we *can* make rational, clearly thought-out decisions about what investment vehicles to utilize, assess the risk-potential - look at our goals, temperament and resources... and come up with a workable plan.

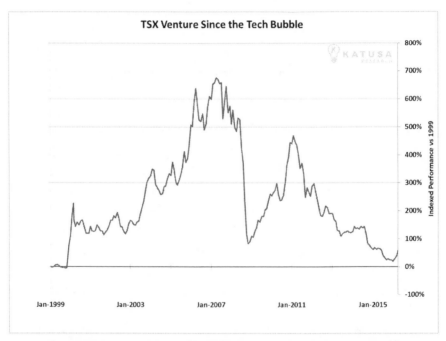

Creative Destruction: the TSX-V (courtesy Katusa Reseach)

It's important to acknowledge at the outset, that resource sector stocks as a group are by just about any measure, one of the most volatile sectors on the board. Doug Casey fondly refers to them as "burning matches" because in order to stay in business, a producer must keep finding new or expanded deposits, since every ounce they mine becomes an ounce less they can depend upon for generating future revenue. By definition, a mine is a wasting financial asset unless it can replace its reserves. (Also because of the way they "burn" through private placement money!)

To make matters worse, the sector goes through massive boom and bust cycles - like the current cycle shown earlier on the TSX-V chart - which, during a boom phase, offer investors some of the most profitable trading opportunities you'll find anywhere. Likewise, during an extended bust, holding most of these companies will offer you a ring-side seat to watch your account balance shrivel like a patch of once-green grass trying to survive in the desert heat.

Some years ago, long time analyst, investor, and newsletter writer, Canadian Bob Bishop, now retired, stated it succinctly, saying: "Until the recent cycle, I never realized what I now regard as the simple truth of resource stock investing: there are times to be in the market, and times to be out of the market. Period."

If down the line, watching your portfolio grow becomes more important than family, friends, fishing, and perhaps even intimacy, recall Bishop's words. He came to that epiphany after going through some wrenching cycles when the miners - all the miners, fell for a very long time. We've done it ourselves.

The primary focus of this book is to help design a plan that keeps you invested for as long as possible during the run-up into a trading mania, offers an "early out" with the majority of your winnings... <u>and</u> helps you to hold onto a "stay in the game" vehicle. Even if you end up withdrawing the majority of your profits "way too early", you'll still be able to work with a tool having the potential to earn another pile of money. The keys? Learn how to construct that vehicle. How to use it. And how to let it go.

Our approach effectively address the psychological and practical aspects of riding the gold and silver bull as long as possible, getting out at a time/place/profit level you decide upon... yet still maintaining a viable position that can take advantage of an unanticipated continuation to the upside.

(Note: This writer - David Smith, participated in the 1974-80 gold and silver bull market, holding physical metal and trading futures. He overstayed his welcome into the spring 1980 top, and while making a profit, gave back <u>way too much</u> during the epic collapse after the Hunt Brothers' silver efforts unraveled.)

Understanding how to avoid such a scenario this time around - and spreading the word as to how it might be done, is one of the "core" reasons this book is being written.

Putting together a 10x, 3 - 5 year precious metals' battle plan!

We're not going to discuss esoteric investments like options, futures contracts, or even stocks on margin. The odds against using these vehicles do not favor longer-term success, except for a few highly-skilled, and sometimes lucky participants.

Rather we look primarily at fully-paid-for resource sector company shares and ETFs. The strategy is to focus mostly on profitable, well-managed operations with a growing production and resource base - plus allow for a limited selection of "prospective" exploration plays located in relatively low country-risk locales. Attempting to buy them into periods of price weakness, will go a long ways towards helping meet your 10x or more goal on as many choices as possible.

The Goal in Holding Mining stocks is wealth creation

After putting into practice the idea of "stacking" some physical gold and silver, which we discussed in Chapter 3, research and consider choosing 5-10 (but no more than 20) producing mining companies.

Even though many of the incompetent companies have dried up and blown away or literally- "gone to pot" - you must still be on guard for "pump and dump" schemes that put in their appearance as soon as a bull trend gets underway. Some, in their behavior are not unlike locusts - they hibernate for years, and come to life when the next upside run gets underway. They consume as much of the current "crop" of unsuspecting investor dollars as possible, then go back to ground again and wait for the next cycle.

Here's an analogy illustrating the point. There's a river in Central Africa that almost dries up every year during the summer, yet when the fall rains commence, it becomes a raging torrent. From the few remaining pools, arise 20 foot long crocodiles who glide silently toward shore, lining up on the hapless young Wildebeest who come down to drink. In an explosion they grab their unsuspecting victims and disappear with them into the depths. Do not become one of those victims! Pay attention, use your brain, go with management teams who have succeeded before, keep position size balanced... and yes, even listen to your gut. Finally - never forget - we are ALL speculators!

What's a Streamer or Royalty, and why are they so popular with investors?

Holding shares in royalty companies or streamers can help you diversify. The Streamer pays a miner up front in exchange for a certain amount of production - usually for the life of the mine (LOM) - which they in turn sell upon receipt at prevailing market prices. Or the miner pays a Royalty company an agreed-upon royalty/ounce in exchange for operating, expansion, or exploration capital, either up front, or doled out over time.

Streamers and royalty companies have usually been able to "de-risk" (lower the risk) these deals, so that they are much safer for shareholders than directly buying individual miner shares, no matter how well run it might be. Country-risk, operational accidents, underperforming assets and acts of God are ever-present risks miners face in their working environment on a daily basis. The only concern for royalties and streamers about all of this, is that they receive on time and as agreed upon, the ounces they have been contractually promised.

Many royalty/streaming companies, having struck excellent deals with producers during the last downturn when equity markets had slammed shut, are going to see these agreements come to fruition in a _very_ profitable way! Regardless of where the mining indices are trading percentagewise from the early 2016 lows when you read this, there is MUCH more potential ahead during the coming years for the sector in general, and for shareholders in particular.

300-500-800% (3-5-8x) phase markers.

- A good time to make some money/recover from the 2011-2015 cyclical bear market.
- Returns of three to eight times take many miners back to 2011 share price levels.
- Upside penetration by gold of horizontal resistance-becomes-support (HSR) levels in hundred dollar increments from $1,500 to and through $1,900.
- Penetration of and successful base-building by gold (via retesting) above $2,000.

- Upside penetration by silver of horizontal resistance-becomes-support (HSR) levels in five dollar increments from $25, to and through $45.
- Penetration of and successful base-building (via retesting) above $50 silver.
- The leading edge of the public mania wave starts building as these upside layers of resistance are successfully penetrated and turned into support. 2017 is most likely the year during which the public recognition/participation phase gets underway.
- New all-time nominal highs in gold (>$2,000) and silver (> $50) usher in even more public involvement, leading to what we believe will be the final and most massive move for the precious metals and associated shares.

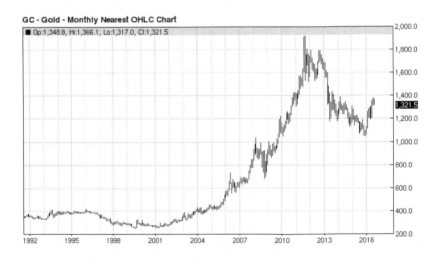

GC - Gold - Monthly Nearest OHLC Chart

Op:1,348.8, Hi:1,366.1, Lo:1,317.0, Cl:1,321.5

Gold 25 year continuation chart courtesy Barchart.com

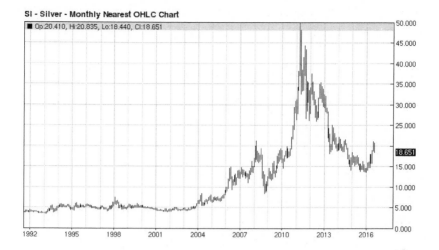

SI - Silver - Monthly Nearest OHLC Chart

Op:20.410, Hi:20.835, Lo:18.440, Cl:18.651

Silver 25 year continuation chart

- As new nominal highs in both gold and silver are printed, several situations begin to develop. Available supplies dry up and precious metals become more difficult to find.
- More counterfeit bullion and "collector" coins and bars circulate in the market place.
- The price, first of gold, then silver becomes elevated to the point that fewer people can afford to buy in quantity. Market supply and premiums expand sharply.
- As the "two steps forward, one step back" bull market progress, earlier buyers begin selling their metal - especially silver - in sometimes significant, but not decisive waves, temporarily slowing silver's rise, <u>creating buying opportunities for dealers.</u>

You might want to take a pass on investing in shares of "Golden Loaves, Inc."

Concomitant with gold and silver's meteoric rise and their problematic availability and affordability, will be an historic rise in the price of mining shares. At some point, "even pigs will fly". In 1980, we heard of a company with the name of something like "Golden Loaves, Inc." that saw its share price - for no reason apparent to the owners - go through the roof. They sold fresh-baked bread, but because the company had "gold" in its name, the attention of ravenous investors with a "taste" for anything gold-like was drawn to them!

The Possibility of Gold Revaluation: Insurance with a BIG Kicker

The U.S. holds an incomprehensible $20 trillion dollar debt, and to all purposes and intents, it looks like both political parties intend to increase it even more!

To top it off, many nations are moving to implement a policy of negative interest rates (NIRP), where the banks charge the customer for the privilege of holding a cash balance! Think about how corrosive this is. While that's going on, the government is actively working to promote inflation - in order to pay its obligations on social security and government pensions in debased dollars - while your purchasing power continues to decline. The result? A double sucker punch to your economic gut.

In Europe, NIRP is causing corporations to begin hoarding cash and buying gold rather than keep a large bank balance. In Japan, home safes to store cash are being purchased in record numbers, demand for 100,000 yen notes is going through the roof and gold purchases have tripled.

Since 2010, central banks have become net buyers of gold.

As the world's governments come face to face with the prospect of currency collapse, something's got to give. Confidence in (acceptance of) fiat money is all that holds things together. Once a run out of a country's currency gets underway - into anything of tangible value -it's game over. Even the ability of banks to suspend redemptions from your money market funds - instituted by federal decree last year - will prove to be nothing more than a metaphorical finger in the dike.

How can central banks around the globe, as it slips into a synchronized recession... or worse, dig themselves out of the approaching monetary-debt abyss without going through a systemic collapse?

There is an answer. Written about, yet scoffed at by virtually every "intellectual" and "economist" who has been asked about it. The "answer" - born of and nurtured through centuries of history in the crucible of economic need? A revaluation in the price of the most powerful, effective, and durable store of value humankind has ever utilized - gold. Talking business heads and politicians like to say, "There's not enough gold!" Yes there is... but only at the right price!

Gold revaluation (not monetization - where gold actually circulates and is redeemable in exchange for paper script as a monetary medium), could be instituted by central banks - perhaps even by the U.S. Federal Reserve.

Revaluating all currencies against gold -"It's eighth grade math."

So far, the world's major currencies have been taking turns devaluing against each other in an effort to improve their country's trade position in the global economy. It's mathematically impossible to devalue all currencies at the same time, so as the "currency wars" intensify, the inevitable result is a spiraling values' race to the bottom. Jim Rickards, in his seminal work, *The New Case For Gold*, shines a light on the way out for these dysfunctional entities, saying:

> ..you devalue it against gold - because gold is money.
> It's not the kind of money that can be printed by a central bank...(but) with gold, everybody can devalue (their currencies) at once...

In order to derive a per ounce dollar figure at which gold needs to be priced to restore public confidence and jumpstart inflation - both of which are central bank goals - Rickards suggests the following formula. First take 40% of global money supply (M1 x 40%), divide this figure by the official gold holdings of the world's central banks (about 35,000 tonnes), and you get $10,000 an ounce as a realistic gold revaluation price. This action would stop deflation - a central bank's worst nightmare - dead in its tracks. And you wouldn't have to reduce the money supply!

Other thinkers, including Anatal Fekete and Hugo Salinas Price, have toyed with a gold figure of between $10,000 and $50,000. Price, long an advocate of using the silver *Libertad* in Mexico as a circulating parallel currency, selects $20,000 as a realistic figure.

He says,

> The discipline of gold as Reserves backing currency
> at a revalued price will restore order to a world that has
> refused to adopt the necessary discipline until forced to
> do so in the desperate situation now evolving, where there
> will be no other alternative but to accept the detested fiscal
> and financial discipline imposed by gold.

Exchanging "paper promises" for real money

The idea of backing a large portion of the floating debt that we have long referred to as "paper promises" looks like it may be moving from a once far-fetched idea toward a deserved place on center stage. You may think that if this happens, you will be able to quickly go to the local coin shop and pick up a handful of metal as soon as the possibility of a gold price rocket launch becomes obvious. But think again. Most likely announced on a Sunday evening, by Monday morning, the precious metals' supply cupboard would certainly be bare. And mining stock share prices would go through the roof. Rickards says,

> Gold will be in such short supply that only the central
> banks, giant hedge funds and billionaires will be able to
> get their hands on any. The mint and your local dealer
> will be sold out. That physical scarcity will make the
> price super-spike even more extreme than in 1980. The
> time to buy gold is now, before the price spikes and before
> supplies dry up.

The "Blue Screen of Death" - with a Silver Lining

Should gold revaluation take place, an important - and almost never considered knock-on effect would be the likelihood for an upward, massive revaluation of silver - as well as gold and silver stocks and ETPs like SIL, GDXJ and GDX, which hold listings comprised of them. Since this has never happened before, we can only speculate about what such an event might look like.

In the fall of 2015, we posted an essay on <u>David Morgan's Blog</u> titled, "Gold and Silver: Heading for a 'Blue Screen of Death' Event?" The analogy compared what can happen when a pc computer hard drive undergoes a catastrophic crash, causing a total loss of stored information, leaving you staring at... a blue screen.

** We should make an important distinction. A silver "blue screen of death" event can take place on its own due to a cataclysmic impact between supply and demand, which could cause a near-simultaneous run to acquire silver- at any price - by both industrial and investment users. (There is a precedent for this - the 2000-2001 palladium run.)

If a gold revaluation - or a series of them - were to take place, you could compress what we write below regarding silver, from weeks and months... to perhaps hours and days.

How a Silver Blue Screen of Death Event Might Look:

It's a Sunday evening...

- In overnight markets, the price of Silver rises $2 – $4 an ounce.
- In extended-hours trading the next morning, silver stock ETFs open 50% higher.
- American Silver Eagles/Canadian Maple Leafs sell out in a few hours.
- Premiums on "junk silver" triple from the previous day's level.
- Local coin shops sell out of physical silver by noon the second day.
- Silver moves up sharply each day and ends the week $15 higher.
- During the week, silver producer shares triple from the previous Friday's close.

- Over the next two weeks, silver retraces just 25% of its meteoric price rise, forming what technicians call a "bull flag". On the third Monday, the "moon shot" continues, easily breaking through multi-year resistance at $38, then $44, and finally the all-time (nominal) highs above $50, closing a few weeks later at $75 an ounce.

- For several months the price forms a broad trading range below a spike high at $80, but is unable to drop below $55 an ounce. Almost no retail metal is available, and when it is, the premium is $15 over spot. Primary silver mine producer stocks trade well above their 2011 highs, in some cases 50 times higher than their bear market low.

- Unlike 1980, silver trading this time is a global phenomenon. Internet news is instantaneous, with Chinese markets setting the price. The COMEX has defaulted on its futures' contracts and settles by paying out with paper promises.

Four months later, silver prints a new all time nominal high and surges into the $125 - $175 range, on its way to $250+ per ounce, in the biggest metals' bull market in modern history. Gold penetrates $8,000 an ounce on the upside.

Note: Even at $125, silver would still be cheaper in inflation adjusted dollars than it was in 1980! Is such a scenario possible? Stay tuned...

The 'Blue Screen' versus a Gold Revaluation?

The 'blue screen event' we've just discussed presupposes simply a supply-demand train wreck silver price moon-shot taking place due to a lock-up in silver supply colliding with a wave of physical metals buying/hoarding. Gold prices would no doubt shoot up too, but it's difficult to quantify how that would play out *vis a vis* silver.

What would be going on, if instead of the *blue screen event* - causing a massive silver price increase in its own right, but which would probably play out over a series of months to a couple of years - an epic event took place <u>overnight</u> (it would be on a Sunday), whereby the world's central banks, in an effort to underpin a portion of the world's paper debt and maintain/restore public confidence, announced a gold revaluation of thousands of dollars the ounce higher?

We can hazard an educated guess about those effects as well....

On the Monday morning following the Sunday night gold revaluation, mining stocks and ETFs would explode upwards, with many producers increasing in value by hundreds of percent in the first hour. Don't forget that beyond a certain price point for the metal they produce, the all-in-sustaining-cost (AISC) of an operation does not rise appreciably, but the effect on bottom line profitability increases enormously. If a miner can produce silver and make a return at $20/ounce and gold at $1,200/ounce, what do you think their profit points would look like if silver trades at $150/ounce and gold at $5,000 - $10,000?

Gold's real value is <u>after</u> the crisis has passed.

Sometimes you hear a remark that "You can't eat gold in a crisis." Well, that's true. But where gold (and silver) really shine is during the period <u>after</u> a currency has been devalued sharply (think Venezuela, Mexico, Argentina) or has collapsed outright (think Zimbabwe and again, Argentina). When the old currency is removed from circulation, your precious metals - which will have retained their pre-revision value - can be exchanged for the new currency.

Ask a Zimbabwean citizen if they would rather have traded one trillion old Zimbabwe dollars (which at one point earlier had been worth $US1.27 each) for a new one, called a "banknote"…or an ounce of gold for $1,400 new U.S. Dollars - one of several international currencies now being used for domestic transactions? Think about <u>yourself</u> some day in a similar situation. (In Venezuela, in late 2016, it was reported that just 1 troy ounce of silver would buy…6 *months* of food, and an ounce of gold - a house!)

Zimbabwe 100 trillion Dollars. Original value - $USD 1.27

Perhaps we cannot hold accountable those who serve themselves first, and us not at all. But we can take it upon ourselves to follow the spirit chronicled in Dr. Janice Dorn and Pat Gorman's inspiring book, *Personal Responsibility: The Power of You*. Maintain your physical and emotional health. Do whatever you can to make yourself independent of the government. Keep some cash outside the bank, but within your reach. Hold physical gold and silver either in direct possession, or in an <u>allocated</u> segregated account. Work to increase marketable skills for which others will pay you. Spend an inordinate amount of time - in any activity you choose - going through the OODA Loop so that you can become more capable of responding in "getting ahead of the event" quickly, efficiently... and correctly.

Hugo Salinas Price is one of Mexico's wealthiest citizens. Two years ago in an open letter to the Greek government, he suggested they mint and circulate a one-tenth ounce silver coin that would trade alongside the euro, or a reinstated Greek drachma fiat currency. It's value would rise with the spot price, and never be reduced. The proposal fell on deaf ears, but the game is not over. (A few years before that he proposed the same idea for Mexico, utilizing the one troy ounce silver *Libertad*. Every Mexican state in the legislative body voted for it, but the central bank turned the proposal down.)

Recently, he had this to say about the financial mess now enveloping much of Europe, even as the same kind of storm clouds build here:

> This is apocalyptic. We are in a terrible mess, and there is no way out without suffering. Apocalypse means prices are going to go haywire. Business is going to stagnate. Unemployment is going to prevail. There is going to be enormous disorder. That's what I see will happen. We are not going to get out of this mess easily. It is going to be painful. One way to avoid pain is to have something you will be able to trade for what you need – and that is gold and silver.

Whom do you believe to be more prescient and trustworthy? Whose advice makes more sense? Hugo Salinas Price? Or the central banker/politician/broker who keeps telling you there's absolutely nothing to worry about...until the message changes over the airwaves on a Sunday night...?

It's About Confidence

As long as people retain faith in the banking system, and what politicians tell them, the charade will continue. Greece's near-default, the Chinese stock market melt-down (where investors were told they could not sell their stocks for six months), cyber attacks which have laid bare the personal information of tens of millions of Federal Government employees, while government watchdog agencies again failed to "connect the dots". How much more will it take?

On Wednesday, July 8 2015, there was a "glitch" - a so called "technical hiccup" on the New York Stock Exchange, the world's largest, forcing a three hour trading halt. The *Washington Post* described it thus:

> So what exactly went wrong?' We're not 100 percent sure. NYSE officials called the problem an 'internal technical issue' early in the day. There are some reports that the exchange was planning to update some of its software Wednesday morning. It may be that those updates went awry...

It may have been a big deal. Or maybe not. What you can be sure of, however, is that "the government" in its infinite wisdom, is not going to tell the truth unless it's in their best interest. Don't forget, that the word "confidence" begins with "con". Time and time again the Federal Reserve, major banks, financial houses and politicians have said one thing at the time, and said or done something else later. We might find out years afterwards, only after lengthy queries through the Freedom of Information Act, that they were lying.

The Authorities understand that once confidence evaporates, the game is over. So they will do and say <u>anything</u> in order to keep the masses believing, all the while lining their own pockets. Study history, and you'll see this is nothing new. People for thousands of years have understood this, and the more alert among them have taken steps to prepare accordingly. Just remember the absolute truth - "Don't fully believe that the government is going to do the exact opposite on something, until they officially deny it." "As a further refinement, expect for the event to occur immediately after the government's third denial."

To demonstrate just how "out of bullets" the Monetary Masters have become, consider what took place in August 2016, at the Jackson Hole, WY Federal Reserve-hosted Economic Policy Symposium. An Economist gave a talk to a rapt audience, proposing a novel way to do what we would describe as "re-characterizing cash." He called it the "flexible market-determined deposit price of paper currency" - the idea that the money in your wallet might have a different "value" than the funds in your bank account. In effect there would be an "exchange rate" between your two forms of "money". The rate would be determined by the Federal Reserve. As Jim Rickards describes the scheme, "It's a way to impose negative interest rates on cash. It sounds like an idea on how to 'split your cash' on the way toward "destroying your cash."

Now you might respond, "Well, that's just someone's idea - it could never become a reality!" Regarding how "ideas" become "reality" - consider that before the fall of Czarist Russia and the rise of the Bolsheviks during WW I, Germany sent an "idea man" - Vladimir Illyich Lenin, from Germany into Russia in a sealed train...

Let these circumstances offer greater assurance that your foray into precious metals and mining stocks makes even more sense than you might have originally thought, or than the naysayers pushing bonds, traditional stocks, term and old age insurance as "less risky", would have you believe. For 11 consecutive years, during which time gold steadily rose, you would have heard the same chorus from the "investment specialists". The next time you're given such advice, ask them "How much gold or mining stocks did *you* buy during that time?"

Yes, there is risk here. But approached in an informed, calculated way - and done with a sensible exit plan in mind ahead of time, it could turn out to be the most remunerative actively upon which you've yet engaged.

A word of caution, which we have mentioned throughout this book, is that no matter how much sense the ideas presented here make to you, it is important to keep your overall financial holdings balanced - in other words do not become a precious metals-only investor.

Not just a "Fear Trade", but also a "Love Trade"

In our discussions, we are not even factoring in either a gold revaluation or a silver "blue screen of death" event into calculations, for the possibility of achieving a 10x return on your portfolio. Absent either or both events, it's still not only achievable, but may well even be a conservative expectation.

Should either of the aforementioned events - gold revaluation or silver blue screen take place, it's almost impossible to calculate what your returns might be from an investment that had a significant position already in place. A modest figure could provide a yield literally off the charts, related to what you might be expecting. Talk about a "profit kicker", eh?

Finally, do not think, as some respond when we speak of the possibility of three-digit silver and four digit "choose-a-first-number" gold, that this automatically means anarchy, chaos in the streets, revolution, or world war. No, simply due to ongoing financial mismanagement on a global scale, and the desire of 3 billion people to have the kind of life style we take for granted, these price levels can still come to pass. Not to mention a production drop-off in the future because of an implosion of mining-funded exploration for new deposits during the last five years. Add the motivational force which for thousands of years has driven people from around the globe and across cultures to hold onto gold and silver as financial life preservers in time of need, and the ensuing demand for precious metals has the potential to swell almost beyond belief.

We can state it no better than did Physicist and polymath Jacob Bronowski, in his *Ascent of Man*, to wit - "Gold is the universal prize in all countries, all cultures and in all ages."

Yes, the day will come when the powerful core drivers of this greatest of all precious metals bull markets begins to subside. When that gets underway, you do not want to remain "all in". You should avoid, as much as possible, ending up the way Jesse Livermore, in his classic *Reminiscences of a Stock Operator*, spoke about the average investor. Said he, *"Money in booms is first made by the public - on paper... and on paper it remains."*

And that, dear reader is exactly what we intend to help you avoid!

CHAPTER 6

A TEN TIMES Your Money 3-5 Year Precious Metals' Battle Plan: Part II

Fear is your best friend or your worst enemy. It's like fire. If you control it, it can cook for you; it can heat your house. If you can't control it, it will burn everything around and destroy you... it makes you more alert, like a deer coming across the lawn. **Mike Tyson**

Over the years, *The Morgan Report* has written several extensive reports dealing with mining and precious metals' Exchange Traded Funds (ETFs). It's no exaggeration when we say this sub-category of ETPs are "double-edged (gold and silver-tipped) swords". In fact the analogy that Mike Tyson and his trainer used when comparing fear to fire is entirely appropriate.

Before we continue our discussion, let's specifically address - not just infer - a very important point. You can go through the rest of this bull market without ever trading a standard configured ETF, let alone a leveraged or an inverse one, and still do very, very well by simply holding specific mining stocks. Achieving a 10x, perhaps even better, is entirely possible. In this chapter, you'll see plenty of caveats to go along with the potential advantages of using ETF/ETPs. This cautionary paragraph - indeed this entire book - is written in the spirit of informing your opinions, rather than attempting to lead them. In the final analysis, the decisions are - and must be - yours and yours alone.

The ETP - What it is and why you should consider using it...carefully

The Term "Exchange Traded Product" (ETP) refers to the universe of such funds, including Exchange Traded Funds (ETFs), Exchange Traded Notes (ETNs), and Exchange Traded Fund Securities (ETFS). In this book, we will generally use of the term "ETF", since it is the one most commonly used by market participants.

With up to 5,000 ETPs listed in the U.S. markets alone, the category is successfully challenging the domain once dominated by mutual funds. Several general statements can be made regarding ETFs:

- ETFs will continue to grow in variety and popularity with investors.
- ETFs have significant structural/performance strengths *and* weaknesses.
- ETFs individual offerings rise and fall subject to investor acceptance and use.
- ETFs' performance during an entire market cycle is yet to be tested, but will surprise investors on both the upside *and* the downside.

What is an ETF?

An Exchange Traded Fund (ETF) is a fund that (generally) tracks an index, but can be traded like a stock. It (generally) does not seek to outperform an index, but rather is "passive" in that it tries to mimic it. The securities found in an index are bundled together so that the ETF can be bought and sold as a unit.

ETFs do NOT track mutual funds, since a mutual fund only discloses its holdings periodically and thus an ETF's stated composition at a given point might lag what the mutual fund was actually holding. Further, an EFT can trade during market hours, literally minute to minute, whereas a mutual fund investor can only buy or sell a fund once a day. Their order has to have been placed during market hours, yet the execution price won't be known until the fund's Net Asset Value (NAV) has been determined - after the market close.

ETF Advantages over Mutual Funds

- You can trade an ETF in a brokerage account.
- You can determine price execution by trading "at the market", "limit" or on a "stop".
- ETF components can be valued daily - Mutual Funds report holdings quarterly.
- ETFs generally charge a lower fee (and are no load) for tracking a given index.
- Investors may go long/short/options with an ETF, but mutual funds are long only.
- ETFs have no minimums, and are more tax efficient than mutual funds.
- You can buy/sell throughout the trading day, taking advantage of a news event before it is fully reflected in the share price of a company within the index.

ETF Cautionary

- *Some* ETPs are closed-end, so their price may be higher or lower than the NAV.
- Not all perform according to expectations.
- Low-volume (poor investor acceptance) ETFs may have wide bid/ask spreads.
- Some may have relatively high management fees.
- ETFs tied to futures rollovers can have problems maintaining expected returns.
- During periods of extreme volatility, the bid/ask spread can widen appreciably.
- Before using an ETF, consult a chart service for daily volume to confirm liquidity.
- Bullion ETPs have counterparty risk. You're relying on operational integrity, management proficiency and the presence of regulatory

oversight. If any of these elements are missing, delays in redemptions/outright default could take place.

Buying and selling shares directly (in large blocks called "creation units") to or from the fund manager can only be done by "Authorized Participants" – usually institutional investors (e.g. banks and brokerage houses) who either invest in the shares themselves or act as market makers, providing liquidity in the open market. Individual investors buy and sell ETF shares in the secondary market through a broker.

Bullion Management Group's Nick Barisheff, in an interview on David Morgan's Master Mind series, noted an uncertain wrinkle about this situation in that the *authorized participant can either buy or borrow the underlying asset.* Nick observed that it can,

> "take the borrowed asset contributed to the ETF, get shares back, sell the shares to the public, and keep all of the money... The problem is that you've got two entities who think they own the same assets - the lender of the assets and the ETF shareholders."

A passing look at ETN's

The exchange traded note (ETN), a relative to the ETF is mentioned here in passing –discussing two examples which may have merit. ETNs are debt obligations similar in some ways to corporate bonds. They are purchased from a broker as would be the case with an ETF, but are subject to the issuer's solvency. If the broker goes under, so does your investment in the ETN. Many are thinly traded, and therefore can have wide bid/ask spreads. While some ETFs are higher priced, they are generally speaking, less subject to system risk than ETNs.

In their wording you may notice, that as a class, ETNs fall into a different risk/reward category than ETFs. The Highlights section of one states, *ELEMENTS are not principal protected. At maturity or upon repurchase, investors will receive a cash payment linked to the performance of the underlying market measure... (investors) may receive substantially less than their original investment in ELEMENTS upon maturity or repurchase by the issuer.*

You can anticipate similar risks if you substitute the name of most ETNs for "ELEMENTS".

A few years ago, one of the ETNs we might have considered was the *PowerShares DB Gold Double Long ETN* (DGP). At one time the volume was more robust, and even more important, the entity backing it, Germany's Deutsche Bank, was a much stronger institution than is now the case. By mid 2016, Deutsche Bank shares themselves were actually trading below their 2008 panic low levels... not a good sign. In fact, we believe that Power Shares has actually stopped sponsoring this ETN, given the perception of Deutsche Bank's questionable financial health.

iShares Silver Trust(SLV) The 800 pound <u>silver</u> ETF gorilla

A decade ago, precious metals investors were given an option, under-appreciated by many at the time - to start trading silver in a new way. In April of 2006, the first silver exchange-traded fund in the U.S, Barclay's iShares Silver Trust SLV (AMEX) appeared on the scene, with an initial deposit of 1.5 million ounces seeded into the trust. SLV was a trading vehicle which gave/gives investors easy access to investment in the silver market. This particular method of investing has been criticized by some, who say that a person generally cannot take silver delivery (true), that it can be short sold (also true), that it may not have all of the silver it claims to possess (worthy of debate), and that there are better ways to "invest" in silver (also true).

Even before SLV came into being, the concept was disparaged by the Silver Users' Association, who claimed (correctly) that it would take a lot of physical silver off the market, thereby helping to drive up silver prices. One jaundiced comment stated that "the proposed silver ETF might be a legal way for investors to squeeze the silver market."

The biggest advantage for silver bulls is that the existence of the ETF universe widens the participation field. It gives the non-traditional investor an easy way to participate within the framework of a regular stock-trading account. They can (especially using a discount broker) trade in a cost-effective way, on a short, intermediate or long term horizon. If and when a true physical metals' squeeze develops, it may become the "last train out" for those who waited too long to acquire hold-in-your-hand physical silver and gold while they were still available.

This vehicle helps institutional investors, who often cannot buy physical silver or a given mining stock for that matter, unless their office has officially recommended it, yet CAN purchase the metal or a stock when it is housed within an ETF. Institutional Investors(on the buy side) provide more power to a bull leg, while exacerbating a downside run – as was the case with GLD gold sales during the 2011-15 cyclical bear market. At the same time, SLV silver holdings were relatively unaffected. Meanwhile, *physical* purchase of gold and silver by individuals went through the roof!

Above all, the purchase of SLV shares translates directly into a drawdown of physical silver supplies, since the fund's custodians must buy metal in the open market. From 2006 – the present, silver's price has been volatile in both directions, but so far, with a firmly entrenched upward bias, SLV holdings have increased at a steady pace.

SLV issues new shares in 50k block increments and uses them to help equalize, on a daily basis, the supply/demand effects of their physical silver holdings, published daily. At this writing, SLV holds over 350 million ounces of silver bullion. The custodians take an annual 0.5% "Sponsor's Fee" of fund's assets to pay for storage, administration and a small profit.

Regardless of how one feels about the transparency of SLV regarding the question, "Is all of the published amount of physical silver actually there?", it is currently *the* prominent ETF in the silver "physical" metals' space.

During the 2008 economic meltdown, while the price of paper silver dropped a third in a little more than two months, SLV holdings hardly budged. This would seem to demonstrate something important, not only in terms of the vehicle itself, but also about the frame of reference of the majority of participants who hold it.

A disadvantage of SLV for leverage junkies, is that it cannot perform much better than that of underlying physical silver bullion - which is the way it was designed. This is where mining stocks and the newer leveraged ETFs come into play.

A philosophical consideration for some investors is that SLV's custodian is JP Morgan. In the past, the company has had lawsuits lodged against it for allegedly manipulating the silver market. It also holds what many consider to be an outsized silver futures short position.

Positive reviews have been penned by others on both the Physical Swiss Gold Trust ETF (SGOL), as well as the ETFS Physical Silver Shares ETF (SIVR). SIVR trades up to 300,000 shares daily and is a step removed from SLV for those who are so inclined.

ETF Considerations/Concerns Specific to the Resource Sector

Not all ETFs for a given commodity are identical. A case in point is the gold ETF category. Some buy and hold physical gold bullion in storage, whereas others invest in futures contracts. A bullion ETF therefore, might be expected to track the price of gold more closely than one holding gold futures. The latter could be influenced when periodic contract rollovers take place, by *backwardation* (nearby contracts trading higher than the distant) or *contango* (nearby trading lower than distant, as well as having to account for interest charges, hedging, etc). Contango, by the way, is the usual (normal) method of pricing for futures contracts. If a commodity trades in backwardation, it may mean that the near-term supply/demand equation is in question, bringing into play the possibly of sharply higher prices in the spot or nearest month..

CEF – an Outlier in an "ETF-like" space

For those who want a "paper-metal" long term hold vehicle – consider the Central Fund of Canada (CEF), around since 1983 – a full 21 years before the first gold bullion ETF was launched (Nov, 2004). It was thus the first gold exchange-traded product. Founded in 1961, it was later reconfigured so that investors could trade it like a stock. It was listed first on the TSX (1966), and later on the AMEX (1986), with the ticker symbol CEF.

CEF is a closed-end fund, meaning that since the number of shares available at a given time are fixed, its share price may trade higher (at a premium) or lower (at a discount) than its Net Asset Value (NAV), depending upon shareholder demand for the limited amount of available stock. (In an open-ended fund, new shares are created by managers to meet current investor demand.)

Periodically, inspections are required to be performed in the presence of both the Central Fund's external auditors and bank personnel. (Fort Knox, are you listening?) As CEF's Chief Executive describes it,

> "Our bullion is stored in separate cages, with the name of the owner printed on the cage, and on top of each pallet of bullion it states Central Fund or Central Gold-Trust. This disables the bank from using the asset from any of their purposes. We also pay Lloyds of London for coverage of any possible loss."

The late Ian McAvity was a Director of Central Fund of Canada Limited in 1983, upon "its conversion to a specialty entity holding physical gold and silver in LBMA 'Good Delivery' bars in segregated, allocated safekeeping in Canadian bank vaults that are audited to create stock-exchange tradable bullion proxy without the mining risks." (source: Ian McAvity's Deliberations on World Markets, 6.14). Note: Until his passing in early 2016, Ian was *still* a Director on the CEF Board!

GLD: The 800 pound golden ETF Gorilla

Several associated gold ETFs are grouped under the name Exchange Traded Gold, sponsored by the World Gold Council. The primary one, which accounts for the lion's share of gold ETF volume within the group was listed on the NYSE in 2004 under the name *streetTRACKS Gold Shares*.

In 2008 it was renamed SPDR Gold Shares/SPDR Gold Trust ETF (NYSE:GLD). It holds gold bullion, with each share representing one-tenth of an ounce of gold. As of mid- 2016, GLD, at over 28.7moz (894 tonnes), was listed as one of the top ten gold holders on the globe.

GLD's Summary Prospectus states:

- "The investment seeks to replicate the performance, net of expenses, of the price of gold bullion. The trust holds gold, and is expected to issue baskets in exchange for deposits of gold, and to distribute gold in connection with redemption of baskets. The gold held by the trust will only be sold on an as-needed basis to pay trust expenses, in the event the trust terminates and liquidates its assets, or as otherwise required by law or regulation.

- "In accordance with LBMA practices and customs, the Custodian does not have written custody agreements with the subcustodians it selects. The Custodian's selected subcustodians may appoint further subcustodians. These further subcustodians are not expected to have written custody agreements with the Custodian's subcustodians that selected them. The lack of such written contracts could affect the recourse of the Trust and the Custodian against any subcustodian in the event a subcustodian does not use due care in the safekeeping of the Trust's gold. See 'Risk Factors—the ability of the Trustee and the Custodian to take legal action against subcustodians may be limited'."

There's a lot to chew on here for those who need assurance that GLD, or any other metals' ETP will remain a functionally-safe vehicle under various market conditions. The simplest strategy - assuming you decide to trade them? Look at them as tactical instruments with short to intermediate term, time-frame holds, not core holdings.

ETFs make up about 25% of equity trading volume during an average market day. GLD attracted thousands of new gold investors were attracted to GLD. Most likely, many have been first time buyers. As more investors are attracted to the ETF platforms, higher prices are in store.

Impressive as GLD's holdings are, they pale in comparison to the open interest, size and trading volume of the COMEX gold futures market.

According to the CME Group:

"Currently, the SPDR Gold ETF trades an average of 24 million shares (GLD) on a daily basis representing 2.4 million ounces of gold. In comparison, the average daily volume for COMEX Gold futures is over 200,000 contracts which equates to approximately 20 million ounces changing hands on a daily basis with an additional 48 million ounces (or 1,366 metric tons) held in open positions. Over 90 percent of these futures contracts are traded electronically."

The market cap at this writing was over $35 billion.

It might be interesting to see if, during silver's up and down spikes, the spread widens enough to trim potential returns of those buying and selling *with* the majority. In regard to GLD, this issue actually *has* been researched and quantified. Frank Holmes of U.S. Global Investors has done the math and can demonstrate that, if bought and sold at inopportune times, GLD will noticeably *underperform* gold itself.

Inverse ETFs – A "Surgical" Trading Tool?

An *inverse* ETF is a specialized investment vehicle which moves in the <u>opposite</u> direction of the security or index it is designed to track. In all other respects, it performs in identical fashion to that of any other ETF. A variety of financial instruments, such as futures and options, can be housed within them, enabling the discriminating investor to perform a number of trading strategies. For the truly courageous, "ultra" inverse funds, utilizing two to three times leverage are available. They can be used to rebalance a portfolio and help control/contain the risk faced by even the most skilled investors – market timing.

One of the first inverse funds to be created was the Rydex Inverse S&P 500 Strategy Inverse Fund (RYURX), known among professionals as the Rydex !ASETRYURX (URSA), or just "ursa" – Latin for "bear". At this writing, the most notable inverse fund existing for shorting silver –is the ProShares UltraShort Silver (NYSE Arca: ZSL). For shorting gold, intrepid investors can choose PowserShares UltraShort Gold (NYSE Arca: GLL).

Keep the concept of the inverse ETF in mind. "There will come a day" when the precious metals bull has grown weary. When that time arrives, "surgical" use of this investment tool might not only hedge a portion of your current long position, but also offer a profit tactic on the downside. Charting history shows that prices tend to fall 3 – 4 times as fast as they rise. More about this later…

Looking at ETFs as "Financially-Explosive Devices" (FEDs)

According to David Stockman, as of late 2016, there were almost 5,000 ETFs (in various stages of financial health), with a combined value of over $3T, and further, most of their exponential growth occurred *after* the 2008 crisis. You can be certain that if/as you're reading this in 2017 and later, the number and growth of this category will be even higher. Stockman refers to them, only slightly in jest, as "financially explosive devices" (FEDs).

This is one more reason, added to the ones we've been discussing, as to why you must consider ETFs as a category, to be speculation vehicles, not buy and hold core holdings.

Discussing an energy ETP with 96 entries, he comments:

> "No long-term investor would possibly believe that such a hodgepodge of industries can be rationally analyzed at the company specific level. After all, the whole point of competitive markets is to sort out the winners, losers at the sector, industry and sub-industry level. So buying the entire industry in a single stock amounts to embracing self-cancelling financial noise. That undoes all the hard work Mr. Market performs at the operating performance level."

When you think of our admonition that ETFs are "double-edged swords, add still another caveat, they can also at times function as "swords without a tsuba" - a Japanese Cross-guard. The cross-guard is a bar (European) or rounded sword-fitting (Japanese) of metal placed at right angles to the blade in order to protect the user's hand.) So, if you decide to use ETFs as trading tools, you now have a "double-edged sword", without a hand guard, comprised of "burning matches". Chances are, this will provide more than enough excitement for you, and hopefully enough potential reward to justify the risk!

ETFs may come and go, but Gold and Silver remain

The website *Invest with an Edge*, at this writing lists 472 ETFs and ETNs being followed on its "ETF Deathwatch". Some of these, not unexpectedly, were precious and base metals funds both bull and bear, though specific country stock indices seemed to be over- represented. The average age of the terminally ill patients on their list runs between

4 and 5 years, so there is a marked tendency towards "slow-death". Some just shrivel up due to a lack of interest (low trading volume), but mostly the departed simply close shop and delist. Even a few years from now, the concept underlying the following comment from their site, will be valid, notwithstanding that the numbers on their watch list may have changed a bit. They write:

> "Nearly 25% (472 of 1,902) of all ETFs and ETNs are now on ETF Deathwatch, and their lack of liquidity continues to be one of the primary concerns. Twenty-four products went the entire month of May without a single trade, and 251 had zero volume on the last day of the month. Trading concerns are not limited to just these ETFs, because many others also have their weak moments. In fact, 725 ETFs (38% of all listings) had at least one zero-volume day in May."

The moral of this story? Before you consider stepping into even the shallow end of the ETP sector pool, check out Daily volume and Liquidity on a particular choice. If either are on the thin side... it could be better not to invest.

You're going to hear this message from us again. ETF's are trading tools, not buy and hold assets. Think of them the way a surgeon does a scalpel. They have a specific function. When that function is not required, this "tool" remains *at* hand, instead of in-hand.

To drive this point home, here's a horror story as recounted at investwithanedge.com:

> "(In April, 2016) the NYSE suspended trading and delisted DB Commodity Long ETN (former ticker DPU) because its assets fell below $400,000. However, DB left shareholders holding the bag because it has no intention of automatically liquidating the ETNs and returning money to shareholders. Adding insult to injury, the notes do not mature for another 22 years. If owners are not willing to

wait that long, then they will have to pursue the monthly round-lot redemption process or a sale in the over-the-counter markets. Keep this in mind before buying one of the 39 other DB-sponsored products that are currently on Deathwatch."

To hang onto *any* ETF thinking you might someday be able to lay claim to the metal represented by the shares held (with the possible exception of one of the Sprott funds), is naïve to a fault. Even if all the metal advertised is there – which many knowledgeable observers question – the bottom line with an ETF, as Mike Maloney says, is that "you're (simply) buying <u>price exposure</u> to gold and silver."

Three "top – tier" ETFs to consider: GDX, GDXJ and SIL

Once your core mining producing holdings have been established, you have the option of adding one or more mining stock-based ETFs to the accumulation/trading model. Several have performed well for this writer. They are GDX, GDXJ, and SIL

The Market Vectors Gold Miners ETF **(GDX)** holds approximately 50 companies (including those found in the HUI – making it an excellent proxy for the latter) engaged in the acquisition, production and exploration of gold properties. It is billed as "a modified market capitalization weighted index comprised of publicly traded companies involved primarily in the mining for gold and silver."

Perhaps even more fascinating, given the propensity of mid-cap producers to outperform (on a percentage basis) the larger producers - while introducing additional volatility, was the introduction of the Market Vectors Junior Gold Miners ETF **(GDXJ)**. Offering exposure to around 48 gold *and* silver miners, this fund was warmly received by the marketplace on Day One – as well as by *this* writer on that very day! Among its top holdings at this time are First Majestic Silver, Alamos Gold, Iamgold, Novagold, and Pretium Resources.

The Global X Silver Miners Fund **(SIL)** debuted in April, 2010. This fund owns a basket (currently) of 22 silver miners with wide geographical dispersion. In the fund's top ten holdings – comprising about 62% of the fund's assets) can be found Pan American Silver, First Majestic Silver, Silver Wheaton, Hecla Mining, and *Industrias Peñoles SAB*. Its relative **(SILJ)** holds both silver producers and explorers, and lists 24 companies.

The "Other White Metals" ETF - "Terminated" February, 2016

Here's another ETF cautionary tale. The "hybrid metal" *ETF, is (was) the ETFS White Metals Basket Trust* **(WITE),** which invested in silver, platinum and palladium. JPMorgan Chase Bank was the original Custodian. In early 2016 the ETF was "terminated" and ceased trading shares. After a certain point, remaining shareholders were required to tender their shares to three different bullion clearing banks - one for each metal! Laggards who wanted to offset, faced the following procedures:

> "...holders who do not have access to all three accounts may wish to sell their Shares prior to the last day of trading on NYSE Arca. Otherwise, these holders will not be able to redeem their Shares, and will not receive any distribution with respect to their Shares until after the Trustee makes a final distribution to DTC and DTC makes a subsequent distribution to the registered holders as described below. Consequently, these shareholders will remain exposed to market movements in the price of silver, platinum and palladium until the Trust's remaining bullion is sold for United States Dollars..."

Short form? Be cautious!

ETFs/ETs Backed by Physical Gold and Silver

Sprott Physical Silver Trust (NYSE Arca: PSLV) Exchange Trust/ ETF is a closed end fund. During its relatively short life (introduced in 2010), it has traded at a premium ranging from 7% - 23% of NAV. It will be interesting to see how the premium fluctuates - perhaps along the lines of what has taken place over the years with the Central Fund of Canada (CEF) - as metals move into the later stages of their secular bull cycle.

The Sprott Physical Gold Trust (PHYS), launched in early 2010, is a physically-backed gold ETF. As stated:

> "PHYS will store the underlying gold bullion at the Royal Canadian Mint, a Canadian Crown corporation that acts as an agent of the Canadian government whose obligations generally constitute unconditional obligations of the Canadian Government. With the launch of PHYS, investors now have the ability to invest in gold bullion stored in a number of physical locations, including the U.S., Canada, UK, and Switzerland."

An ETF "Hidden Advantage"

Some readers may hold a precious metals mutual fund, such as (for the purpose of example only) Vanguard (VGPMX) or U.S. Global Investors (USERX). In certain situations, being able to trade ETFs may offer the quick-witted investor a "hidden advantage".

Let's suppose a major company within one of these funds experiences either some very positive or very negative news. If you only hold that company as part of a mutual fund, you would not be able to take quick action to either benefit (from the good news) or side-step (the bad news) until the end of the market session at the earliest. But if you could find an ETF which also held that stock, you might be able to trade it and either capture a larger profit from a company's upside move, or lessen your loss if the target experienced a sharp plunge. (And of course you could also buy/sell the stock.)

The "Fab Four" <u>Leveraged</u> and Inverse metals' ETPs.

In the interest of simplicity, ease and past experience, this writer focuses primarily on the following four leveraged ETPs: **USLV, UGLD, NUGT** and **JNUG**. Their mirror images are **ZSL, GLL, DUST,** and **JDST.** (in late 2016, the most popular commodity-leveraged ETF is probably the triple-leveraged, Silver USLV, with daily volumes in excess of 3 million shares, followed by the double-leveraged Silver AGQ, with volume running between 500k - 1.25m shares a day.

Silver on Steroids: AGQ (2x) and USLV Pro Shares Ultra Silver (3x Long Silver)

In December 2008, the first leveraged and inverse ETFs designed to track the price of silver and gold were introduced by ProShares – part of ProFunds Group, possibly the world's largest manager of leveraged and inverse funds. They were: ProShares Ultra Gold (UGL); ProShares UltraShort Gold (GLL); ProShares Ultra Silver (AGQ), and ProShares UltraShort Silver (ZSL). As ProShares states matter-of-factly, "Use them to magnify the impact of your investment dollar."

Definition/Goals: "ProShares Ultra Silver seeks daily investment results, before fees and expenses, that correspond to two times (2x) the daily performance of silver bullion as measured by the U.S. Dollar fixing price for delivery in London."

The performance just approximates underlying silver prices, though in this writer's experience, it tends to be "close enough". The proshares.com site expresses the possible deviation thus:

> "This Ultra ProShares ETF seeks a return that is 2x the return of an index or other benchmark (target) **for a single day**, as measured from one NAV calculation to the next. Due to the compounding of daily returns, ProShares' returns over periods other than one day will likely differ in amount and possibly direction from the target return for the same period. These effects may be more pronounced in funds with larger or inverse multiples and in funds with volatile benchmarks. Investors should monitor their holdings consistent with their strategies, as frequently as daily. For more on correlation, leverage and other risks, please read the prospectus."

USLV weekly (courtesy Stockcharts.com)

USLV - Pro Shares Ultra Silver (3x Long Silver)

Definition:

> "The VelocityShares 3x Long Silver ETNs linked to the S&P GSCI® Silver Index ER (the "ETNs") are senior, unsecured obligations of Credit Suisse AG ("Credit Suisse") acting through its Nassau branch. The ETNs seek to provide long exposure to three times (3x) the daily performance of the S&P GSCI® Silver Index ER (the "Index") plus a daily accrual equal to the return that could be earned on a notional capital reinvestment at the three month U.S. Treasury rate as reported on Bloomberg under ticker USB3MTA, less the daily investor fee. The ETNs are intended to provide traders with an exchange traded instrument enabling them to efficiently express their market views on the COMEX silver future."

A few years ago, AGQ had higher trading volume, but as of this writing USLV has been notching some 3-4 million + share days. It may well become the new darling of the go-for- broke crowd, some of whom have probably already done so trading silver futures!

As you might imagine, the volatility of this "triple warmer" can be a sight to behold when silver decides to gallop towards the horizon on one of its periodic moon shots - or tanks on a reaction. So be sure to stay on the right side of its trajectory! The bid/ask spread is generally just a few basis points- although it can widen - so it's a good idea to use a limit order unless one has access to real-time quotes.

An effective tactic is to position on the lower edge of deep support (or a break of support if the trader believes it might be a bear trap). Then, if correct, ride the move for some quick profits. If the market moves against the trade, by using good money management, offset the position. The key in limiting losses with any leveraged ETF, is to get out quickly if the trade starts going against you.

A potentially profitable "get ahead of the crowd" trade comes to mind. Suppose an investor holds a favorite low cost of production junior silver producer. Silver goes into an unexpected short-term price spike. If an investor is holding USLV, it might be possible to capture the additional value represented by silver's up-move, sell the ETF, and purchase more shares of the junior miner before it too reflects the higher silver price.

Another tactic is to buy an extended range breakout (or using the Ultra Short Silver ZSL, sell a suspected intermediate top). If the rise turns into a bull trap, offset the highly-liquid position, back to cash. If the trader's analysis and actions are close to matching the market's behavior, this tactic can be undertaken simply, effectively and decisively.

A case can be made that the vehicle which most closely tracks the silver price is not an ETF at all, but rather a stock – the *uber*-streamer Silver Wheaton (SLW). Of course the allure of using USLV, is that its movements come in at around *triple* those of silver itself.

JNUG - Gold Miners Index Bull 3x

The last bull ETF we're profiling here is the Direxion Daily Junior Gold Miners Index Bull 3x (JNUG), and its bearish relative (JDST), trading on the AMEX. (You can learn more about the Direxion family of ETPs by going to direxioninvestments.com)

This is, in part, what Direxion has to say about JNUG:

> "These leveraged ETFs seek a return that is 300% or -300% of the return of their benchmark index for a single day. The funds should not be expected to provide three times or negative three times the return of the benchmark's cumulative return for periods greater than a day.

> "The MVIS Global Junior Gold Miners Index is a cap-weighted total return index. It covers the largest and most liquid small-cap companies that derive 50%+ from Gold or Silver mining or have properties to do so. Companies must have $1 million ADTV [Average Daily Trading Volume], $250,000 shares/month and $150+ million market cap. The cap weight is limited to a maximum of 8% per company; the index is reviewed quarterly. As of June 30, 2016 the average market cap of the index was $1.01 billion and the median market cap was $929 million."

NUGT Weekly (courtesy Stockcharts.com)

NUGT- Direxion Daily Gold Miners Bull 3x Shares ETF...and DUST

Definition: *"The Daily Gold Miners Bull 3x shares seek daily investment results, before fees and expenses, of 300% of the price performance of the NYSE ArcaGoldMiners Index ("Gold Miners Index"). There is no guarantee the fund will meet its stated investment objective."*

The comments made about USLV apply in equal measure to NUGT, the only difference being that its volatility has to do with gold mining stocks rather than the price of physical gold itself. NUGT has been favorably received by certain segments of the investment community, often trading 7 million shares in one day, with spikes exceeding 12 million. During its relatively brief history, NUGT has undergone several reverse splits. Its mirror image on the short side is DUST – appropriately named for what it might do to your acct balance, should you be holding it during a major bull run in the gold mining stocks!

An ETP caveat:

During periods of extreme market volatility...as experienced several times, ETFs can – because of buy/sell demand imbalances - trade at either a discount or a premium to their net asset values. Thus when a trader/investor is "on the wrong side of the trade" – selling into a steep decline/buying into an upward price spike – the result can be, as Barron's Brendan Conway states that "at the very moment of maximum selling, the ETF exacts the maximum trading cost from the seller (and rewards the buyer similarly, with a discount)." Hammering his point home, Conway concludes: "Don't sell into a panic. ETFs are built to penalize lemmings and reward contrarians."

Review of ETP Operational Considerations:

Where we're going with this discussion is that carefully selected and traded "metals ETFs" *can* (not must) interface with a portfolio, such as *The Morgan Report* Asset Allocation model, in one or more ways, in order to:

- Increase portfolio returns
- Increase resource sector trading flexibility

- Multiply the magnitude (profitability) of an underlying metal's move.
- Minimize effects on the overall portfolio due to "bad news" by a company.
- Enable a single trade to participate in the price moves of a number of companies.
- Offer time to pay attention to core holdings while trading other companies.
- Satisfy the urge to "sell/buy something" during rallies/declines.
- Mentally "compartmentalize" Core Holdings for long-term profitability.

Conclusion:

ETFs should be looked upon as a <u>highly specialized trading tool.</u> Their use cuts both ways, especially so in the case of leveraged and inverse ETFs. During the coming public mania, they can play a powerful, highly-focused role in multiplying profits for the investor who is knowledgeable and willing to accept the increased risk their use represents.

- Evidence indicates that ETPs as a category have become a permanent part of the investment landscape, continuing to eat away at what was once the sole purview of the mutual fund industry. Learning how to use ETPs in the context of metals and miners will enable you to appreciate and successfully approach their use in virtually any other sector, from bio tech to homebuilders to rhodium. Approached sensibly, this tool, <u>for the most part</u>, makes consideration of mutual funds, a thing of the past.
- Expect a continued flow of new/refined products designed to offer investors alternative and nuanced ways to make a profit/protect a position in "paper" precious metals and resource sector mining stocks. In addition, expect to see entries not favored by the market shrivel and disappear.
- During market turns, use of Leveraged ETFs offers the potential to realize outsized returns substantially greater than movement of the underlying metal or stock itself.

- Leveraged ETFs holding a basket of companies like those in NUGT (long side) and DUST (short side) can limit (hedge) the risk inherent in choosing one or more of the ones within that ETF. Even a "good company" can blow up or be nationalized.

- When technical analysis indicates price support or resistance is likely to hold, a two or three ETF position (e.g. AGQ/USLV, NUGT), with a close stop near the support zone offers an easy in/out trade, should the perceived boundaries not hold.

- Given the massive volatility now inherent in trading futures contracts, ETFs offer a margin-like,(leveraged) velocity alternative unlikely to decimate ones' account – at least not all at once!

- Keep an eye on the financial strength of the entity backing an ETP you're trading. A few years back this writer often traded the Deutsche Bank's Double Gold Long ETN (NYSE: DGP). Not so today!

- Leverage cuts both ways – hence the term "Double-Edged Sword." These ETFs should *not* be thought of as core holdings. They are a sharp-edged gold (and silver) plated tool -handled as carefully as one would a sportsman's game knife.

- One tactical trading caveat, which this writer (David Smith) has found out through small-scale experimenting with the inverse ETFs mentioned. It is extremely difficult to go against the major trend, whether it's up or down. It's tricky with mining stocks, and it's three times (!) as difficult with leveraged and inverse trading vehicles. Our advice to you is to determine the major trend, then use the opposite-leaning ETPs carefully - if at all. Some highly-skilled traders use them as hedging mechanisms to protect some of their core holdings. For most investors/traders, trading against the major trend will be more complicated than it's worth. The exception might be to include their use within the confines of the special portfolio tool we'll be discussing in greater detail in a few chapters.

- As the price points of EFFs become extended from where they now are, the issue of "counterparty risk" - in extremis, will the financial backers of an ETF default? - is something of which to be aware. In a massive move in one direction or another, an ETF backer might default on its obligation, in which case the EFT holder could lose their investment by definition. (We quoted David Stockman earlier. Be sure to keep this difficult to quantify possibility within the parameters of your expectations model.)

At the risk of beating this point to death, we include another caveat involving gold leasing to/for some ETFs. This doesn't mean that you should not use them, just that it's important to constantly remind yourself as to the advantages <u>and</u> the pitfalls of doing so. First we have the "Guidelines" section of an IMF Issue Paper followed again by Nick Barisheff, regarding how an ETF which leased its gold rather than owning it outright could get into problems, with profound consequences to shareholders. The IMF paper mentions that the monetary authority makes gold deposits,

> "...to have their bullion physically deposited with a bullion bank, which may use the gold for trading purposes in world gold markets" and "the ownership of the gold effectively remains with the monetary authorities, which earn interest on the deposits, and the gold is returned to the monetary authorities on the maturity of the deposits.
>
> As a result, the monetary authorities still show the leased gold as their asset—that is why it is called "leasing." While the gold ETF does in fact have gold in its vaults, the ultimate ownership may be with a central bank. At some point, an AP somewhere in the world, on some ETF, will become insolvent and then the lawyers will get rich arguing who is the rightful owner of the underlying asset—the ETF, or the original lender of the assets? While the litigation drags on, investors' assets will be frozen to the NAV calculated at the time of the default of the AP. Even if the true ETF owners are successful in recovering their capital, this could be a significant lost opportunity cost in a rising gold market. If they are not successful, and it is more likely that the true owner—the central bank lender—will be successful, the 'gold' investment that they made to protect their portfolio would be worthless."

"Don't be wrong like some of the billionaires who have the right concept but the wrong execution in their gold investment—be sure to acquire physical bullion and store it on an allocated, insured basis." - *Nick Barisheff*

The Bottom line: Like any specialized tool, leveraged ETFs can sometimes be just the ticket when market conditions allow. The key lies in knowing when they should be used…and when they should be left alone.

Now that we have done some thinking (and research) as to what our resource-sector trading tool-kit might contain, it's important to clarify what kind of thinking - and execution process - might give us the best chance going forward to reach… and perhaps wildly exceed, our financial goals…

CHAPTER 7

Special Chapter for Americans: Trading Canadian Miners on the Pink Sheets

Times like these try the souls of speculators... and lay the foundation for great wealth, for those with the courage to act and endure. **Louis James**

Once upon a time, there was a Canadian-based mining exploration company listed on the Toronto Stock Exchange named Aurelian Resources (ARU:TSXV). In 2004, it was conducting a drill program on its Condor Project, located in the eastern foothills of the Ecuadorian Andes. With a relatively small share base, its stock was trading below .50 cents/share.

Things were pretty quiet at the time, as evidenced by the following news release the company made on April 19:

TORONTO, ONTARIO--(CCNMatthews - Apr 19, 2004) - Aurelian Resources Inc. (ARU:TSXV) is pleased to announce resumption of its diamond drill program at the Bonza-Las Peñas zone of the Condor Project in southeastern Ecuador. Details of the diamond drilling to date can be found at www.aurelian.ca.

Aurelian's model for the Bonza-Las Peñas zone is a potentially bulk-mineable open pit target with encouraging grades and widths over more than a half kilometer strike length. Additionally, surface sampling and drilling indicate that there are higher grade areas within the zone. The goal of drilling

CHAPTER 8

Good-Bye Mr. Market: The Case for Leaving the Party Early

In the United States problems of economic understanding have been compounded by the effect of economic prosperity. The Japanese in WWII spoke ruefully of 'shoribyo' or 'victory disease'. The Greeks called it 'hubris, and thought it always ended in the intervention of the goddess Nemesis. That lady makes her appearance when wave-riders begin to believe that they are wave-makers, at the moment when the great wave breaks and begins to gather its energy again.- **David Hackett Fischer**, The Great Wave, Price Revolutions and the Rhythm of History

Due to the ineptitude of the money "Maestros" on a global scale, it's highly probable at some point that we will be facing a massive asset destruction unrivaled in history. We're not just talking about inept central bankers, but management at many of the largest commercial banks in the developed and developing world, kleptocrats on Wall Street, and the New Mandarin Class. who legislates for their benefactors, and hence for their own benefit. Not to be left out, legions of "little people" in our midst flip real estate, take out 72 month car loans and deep-dip into college financing unlikely ever to be repaid.

We believe 2008 was only the first of a series of financial tsunamis to hit our shores. The next and more devastating shock-wave is headed our way as you read this book. It will strike with unimaginable force, bringing with it a mass of additional financial flotsam, containing all the unresolved systemic issues, un-payable debt instruments, and "bad bank" assets sequestered by the Federal Reserve and banks in the Eurozone after the first financial tsunami in 2008 breached and almost leveled the walls of the world's monetary sandcastles.

Not only will entire asset classes be destroyed, along with the confidence that underpins the whole system, but something else will be taking place. This fundamentally transformational process is going to shift great wealth from one group of people to another. From the unprepared masses, to the much smaller group who have taken steps beforehand, such as many of those reading and acting upon what is being described in this book.

"To know and not act is the same as not knowing."

This old Chinese saying fits those who realize what needs to be done to place themselves on the right side of the financial change-wave, yet through inertia, laziness or lack of commitment, fail to act. So, don't read this book and then fail to make a plan - any plan that activates the energy and resources you'll need to tackle and take advantage of what's coming your way. Before the market takes it from you.

There is a strong case to be made of selling into strength and "leaving something" for the next buyer. Anyone who has ever traded the futures market has probably learned this lesson the hard way. Professionals strive to buy in the bottom twenty percent of the market and exit within twenty percent of the top. This is sage advice and will serve you well, especially this time, because the amount of emotion surrounding the precious metals as they make their final assent will be almost impossible to resist!

Don't let your wealth-carriage turn into a pumpkin

It is our experience that the precious metals, more than any other asset, seem to invoke a "hold onto" philosophy, no matter how you look at it. When prices explode toward those final, convulsive highs, the metals "bugs" will be mesmerized with how fast their account is growing, not considering how quickly it can shrink when the market finally turns.

When the bell tolls for this historic run, the trading accounts of many investors will head back to or below where they started. Profits will rapidly evaporate during the first sickening leg down of the new metals' Bear Market. Holding on, waiting for new highs, they will instead see the charts begin to print out lower highs and lower lows - the classic form of a good market "gone bad". We hesitate to state with one-hundred percent conviction exactly how the future will reveal itself. The thing is, when the precious metals do become overvalued, we may hear seemingly supportive long-term news, such as rumors about a nation- state going back to some type of gold standard. Regardless, our purpose is to make certain that the reader knows how to measure value - indeed how to get a handle on determining value in relation to price - and why it is so important to understand that at some point, profits need to be locked in.

What if silver runs to $400 (anything is possible), then drops to $30 and finally establishes a "new normal" at $50? If you're in the ranks of the perma-bulls after such a run, you may have made good money, but that's one heck of a profit to leave on the table! Worse yet, what if your average all-in cost was $80? It doesn't have to be this way, but for most investors, that is exactly how the story is going to unfold.

You may have been a gold bug before 2000; perhaps as far back as the 1970's. This time around, you may have established and nurtured big share positions in the 10 best performing mining stocks on the board. You may have "stacked" a small mountain of silver bars and gold coins. But if you don't take certain actions before the clock strikes midnight, you're running a grave risk of watching your wealth carriage of huge profits from these efforts turn into a pumpkin on wheels... or worse.

Sellers Remorse

You've probably heard the term "buyer's remorse". Imagine what it must feel like when you get out of a stock "too early" - and it rockets upward, teasing you to get back in again for the possibility of life-altering gains. Or making you so fearful that you watch the whole run from the sidelines. It can be every bit as painful (and "loss-of-profitable") as getting out too late. Most of those reading this probably had such an experience on at least one occasion. Holding Apple Computer stock for years as you watch it go from $12 - $75 - $15. Getting bored, afraid, finding "a better stock" to buy, selling all of your Apple shares. Seeing it rise by hundreds of dollars a share over several years... while you watched.

We know of an individual who held a large number of shares of the exploration company, Seabridge Gold (NYSE: SA) at $0.43 cents. After a few years of boredom, the stock rose to $0.95 cents and seeing the chance for better than a double, he sold his position and went about other things. Shortly afterward, the stock began a 5-year march... to just under $40.00.

"The big money in booms is always made first by the public - on paper . . . and remains on paper" Jesse Livermore.

Don't forget, it works both ways. At one time you might have owned a large U.S.-based gold and silver producer. You might have bought it for a $1. When it went to $40, you might have held on "for the long term", expecting it to end up at $100. It tried to fund a $1billion plus mine expansion in Nevada while earning a fraction of that in revenue. In a tight-money environment and a multiple-year metals' bear market, it could not. So the share price of that $40 company went to... zero.

Early in the new millennium's secular gold and silver bull market, Silver-Investor.com (now, *The Morgan Report*) recommended a Spokane-based mining company with a property in western Montana holding potentially 260 million ounces of silver. At the time, in late 2002, shares of the company were going for about $0.35 cents apiece. Within less than two years, it had risen to $8, dropped below $4, built a base, and then surged over the next two years to an all-time high slightly in excess of $10/share. We recommended a stop sell at $8 and nearly everyone who followed that call made money. The 2008-09 global near-melt down took it to $0.48; thereafter prices rose to $4.44, then in late 2015, it almost bit the dust at...$0.11 cents. In early 2016, a Major mining company took it out for around $0.80 cents a share.

However, the buy and hold crowd got in early, and held on "for the long term." They watched it rise to $10, crater to .48 cents, and finally waste away to .11 cents. At this point, no doubt many investors bit the dust, selling out their long-suffering positions before it rose a bit and became a buy-out property. Would the kind of portfolio - and the attention we're going to suggest giving it -involving just this one stock - have helped an early shareholder hold onto, and keep a big chunk of those gains somewhere along the line, from .35 cents to $10, and then to .11 cents?

Your assignment, should you decide to accept. Read about the portfolio setup we describe later on in *Second Chance*, and think about what we suggest as a way of handling the rest of this precious metals' bull market. Then return to this page, look at this company's price range over 20 years, and by application through example, construct and "back test" a paper trade position using these numbers which would "float your boat" in the stormy price seas through which this stock sailed before it almost foundered, and was finally bought out.

We could have chosen a number of other mining companies who have had this kind of pricing history. Is there a way to avoid "sellers' remorse" and stay in the game in a meaningful way, in order to have a shot at these gains? Or conversely, to avoid being wiped out by keeping your entire position, riding prices over the top and holding on all the way to the bottom? Of making very big money... on paper, and keeping from giving it all back?

When We Get Close to the "Ultimate Top". The closer we get to the "ultimate top" in this historic silver and gold bull run - and we'll only know for sure in retrospect that it really has been logged - the more difficult it will be, not only to accept that it's starting to move against us, but also to begin taking steps to get off the bus. It won't matter how much you've thought about this event, how much your resolve has been steeled to go through with the plans you laid out years before, how much you attempt to wall yourself off from the cacophony of opinions, data, "proofs" and guru grunts coming from the "experts".

Like the Greek adventurer Odysseus and his crew as they sailed home following the Trojan War, it's going to be easier said than done to resist the Sirens as, during the emotional storm at hand they seek to dash your investment ship on the rocks of indecision, greed, adversity, hubris, second-guessing and fight-or-flight behavior.

It's analogous to how people respond when they find themselves under a deadly threat. They lose fine motor skills, experience tunnel vision as they hear and see only what's directly in front of them, decide to either fight, flee... or freeze in place. Recall once more from our first chapter, the words of Dr. Alexander Elder, in his insightful discussion of what it's like to compete in the investment war space. It consists, he says, (of) *"battling crowds of hostile people while paying for the privilege of entering the battle and leaving it whether dead, wounded or alive."* You experience this when establishing a portfolio of stocks and ETPs, when you add a position, and most certainly when/if you decide to "leave the party early" by going mostly, or all to cash. After that point, strongly consider taking a nice, long rest away from the markets - easily paid for by a portion of your earnings from the historic meals' bull market finale that now lies ahead of us.

It won't be easy to sell a stock you bought at $1 when it's gone to $45, and you're reading that it's destined to rise to $150. Like Novagold (NG), a stock that rose from $0.09 cents to $22.00 back in 2006. At the time, it was a rumored take-out candidate of Barrick Gold. Several analysts penciled the math, showing the company's worth to be "at least $75 a share". But $22 was about it, and when the global financial system almost fell apart in 2008, Novagold dropped to...$0.36 cents. This writer knows about it, because he was watching the markets on that fateful day. Since he was "all-in" with other mining stocks, having been "catching falling knives" on the way down into the fall months - therefore having no extra cash to deploy, he did not take a position. Just two years later that .36 cent stock traded for...$15.00!

As Bob Moriarty says in his excellent little book, *Nobody Knows Anything: Learn to Ignore the Experts, The Gurus and other Fools,*

> "...it makes a lot more sense to take money off the table when you can. Have a plan. Have any plan, but take some money off the table." And, "If you won't walk away when you are winning, the only alternative is that you will walk away when you are losing."

Finally this quote, wherein Bob speaks directly to the conundrum involving the joy and pain our book addresses - and lends support to the underpinnings of our central thesis:

> "I believe silver, gold, platinum, palladium and rhodium are going to go into a bubble that will make the NAZ stock market bubble of 2000 look like a Monopoly

game. And the people who will lose the most money will be the bulls. Because they will never take money off the table. They always want to keep betting. Eventually the house odds win out and they lose it all."

We hope to be establishing in your mind the absolute need of heading to the exits before the rush, along with the rationale that can help best accomplish it, while looking at what some of those exit markers might be.

The Case for Leaving the Party Early

At some point down the line, the precious metals' run which began shortly after the turn of the century will move into its final innings as more and more people jump on the bandwagon in fear – not because they are risk-averse, but because they are just plain scared of missing out.

The premise of this chapter is that <u>relatively few</u> investors who buy gold, silver and the miners during this long-term secular bull market – especially from here on in - will be able to both make <u>and</u> keep a significant amount of money. Countless traders will spend weeks, months and years buying, plotting, counting and holding. They'll "buy the dips", adding to positions, thinking they can pick the top, or profit from the advice of market seers who claim they can call it.

Still others will buy low, but succumb to the plague of movement traders – going all in and all out to play the swings, adding more at a higher price, compromising their average cost per share in relation to the risks they're taking. Greed overwhelms early good sense, as caution is thrown to the wind, because "(surely) this time it *is* different." As prices move into new high ground they experience a burst of euphoria, feeling their stomachs churn, losing sleep with each reaction as the primary bull trend plays itself out. When valuations explode toward their final, convulsive highs, they will be mesmerized with how rapidly their account is growing, not considering how fast it can shrink when the market heads south.

When the bell tolls for this historic run, the accounts of most investors will head back to or below where they started. Profits will rapidly evaporate during the first sickening leg down of the new metals' Bear Market. Market seers will counsel "buy the dip", because it has worked that way every time since the last epic bull run began in early 2016. Only this time, it will be exactly the <u>wrong</u> thing to do!

Holding on, waiting for new highs, they will instead see the charts begin to print lower highs and lower lows - the classic form of "a good market gone bad". Being on the right side for so long, they forget that all parties must one day come to an end. Ignorant of history, they will not heed the words of Baltasar Gracian, the 7th Century Jesuit priest who warned,

> "Place your winnings under cover when they are sufficient or large. Fortune soon tires of carrying anyone long on her shoulders."

We may not see silver trade again at $5 or $10 an ounce…but then you never know! What happens if someday, nanotechnology applications become the norm in the industry for "all things silver"? Or "mining meteors" becomes a viable project? What if silver can be replaced less expensively with something else? Remember Kodak?

We have visited several countries on the globe where historic mining has removed over 1 billion ounces of silver from the earth's crust. It is highly probable that another billion - or two - ounces of silver still remain in those areas, waiting to be discovered and brought to market. In Peru. In Argentina. In Mexico. In Yukon… just to name four. Yes, we are "running out of silver" - at a certain price. If/when we hit $150 silver, or - choose a number - do you realize how much sub-50 grams/ton silver ore will have suddenly become "economic"?

There are massive amounts of gold in sea water, but (at this writing) the technology does not exist to make it economically feasible to produce it. Will that always be the case?

What Jerome Smith Missed

Don't forget the last time "it was different". In 1980, Jerome Smith, the silver guru of that era, wrote convincingly that the world was "running out of silver". But he was only partially correct. It was "running out" based upon the way it was being mined when he was writing. Over the next two decades, a new methodology of metals mining - heap leaching - came to the fore. This process was fated to bring to market hundreds of millions of additional ounces of silver per year.

Silver that Jerome Smith did not factor into his thinking, because he could not have known about this revolutionary and cost effective way to locate and produce silver - mostly as a byproduct of base metal production - that was destined to blow apart his statistical model. Every investor who believed and invested in silver ended up disappointed, because even sound analysis can reach an incorrect conclusion when a paradigm shift (new technology) takes place.

Think about the current bull-run in platinum and palladium. An *avant-garde* company with big money backing is looking at mining in outer space. They say that some meteors contain more platinum than has ever been mined – on earth. If this kind of resource harvesting becomes available down the line, you can bet your last silver dollar that it *will* have a game-changing impact on the price of PGMs mined underfoot on terra firma!

Today, a few forward-looking companies are using down-hole cameras to visually inspect a drill hole - twice as fast and at a 75% savings to the old way. They're using drones and hyper-*spectral imaging* to reconnoiter large swaths of "prospective properties" -a process that used to cost millions of dollars, but now can be done for a few thousand.

The drones are looking for volcanic massive sulfides ore deposits. VMS's are associated with and created by volcanic events on or under the sea floor. These companies are doing what used to take months or years and cost millions, if not tens of millions of dollars to drill and infill. These new methodologies hold the promise of finding mineral rich collections of copper, zinc, lead, gold and silver, not to mention other more esoteric but in-demand minerals present as by - or co-products of the primary mineral field. New resources are being located at a fraction of the cost, in a much-reduced time-frame.

An exploration play in Argentina correlates mountains of data sourced from satellite, aerial and historical surveys. Using proprietary algorithms, the geo team pulls the data together and isolates mineralized zones - some only a few meters across - before putting boots on the ground for additional confirmation via sample collection. Expect more of the same in this sector.

A paradigm shift is under way. There's another epic consideration that has much less to do with how much gold and silver we can find, but everything to do with the tectonic changes brought about due to the closing of what has been termed *The Fourth Turning* by two prescient historians. We'll discuss this transformational idea in our last chapter. Like the authors, we can't predict exactly how it's going to turn out, but we are able to say beyond a shadow of a doubt, that things *will* change across the board, to the point of instituting a new paradigm!.

Hopefully we step through a world door opening into a much better way of doing things for the largest number of people. Whatever the result, we can also guarantee that those changes - one way or another - will have a massive, transformative effect on your gold-silver holdings, and your mining stock portfolio...

We are some years away from this state of affairs, but trees don't grow to the sky. You have to admire those who took the risks, bought when others said the bull market was over, spent endless hours researching the best mining plays, and patiently waited for their "ship to come in". Please remember though, that ships also *leave* the harbor.

A look at the Past: Silver Anniversary, 1980

It was the spring of 1980. This young Grasshopper had gone to an investment conference in San Francisco - the only one he attended during the historic bull run of the 1970's. There would be several dozen speakers promoting products designed to help attendees beat the rate of inflation, then running at over 13%. T-Bills posted record yields. Russia had invaded Afghanistan. Earlier in the year, gold rocketed to an unimaginable $850 per ounce and silver had knocked against $50.

By conference time, the price of silver had backed off into the mid $40's. On *Commodity Perspective* technical charts, an incredible picture was emerging. **Three** distinct and identical trading formations were visible. Each had a price island reversal at its apex, with successive triangles a bit lower than the last. An Island Reversal is a one or two day price range that trades beyond the price action on either side, leaving price gaps. In a top area, prices gap up, trade for one – three days, then gap back down.

Except in thinly traded markets even a single island is rare, but for the technician following a liquid market, an Island Reversal can be one of the most telling formations in charting. (These "islands" in early 1980 were actually a series of limit up and limit down dots, a chart picture that to this day, this writer has never seen duplicated.) If the gaps are not filled within a few days, it is highly probable, at the very least that an intermediate top is in place. Such an extreme reading can hold for a long time. In the case of silver, these reversals created a price top lasting over 30 years. Could this happen again?

Harry Browne Speaks The first speaker was Harry Browne. He had written the prescient texts, *How You can Profit from the Coming Devaluation* (1970), and *How to Profit From a Monetary Crisis (1974)*, wherein he spelled out his view about the price adjustments that would occur as a result of the failing U. S. monetary policies of his day. His prediction of massive increases in the price of gold, silver and the Swiss Franc had come to pass. At one time he had worked for Jerome Smith. He was by all accounts, the most widely-followed silver analyst in the world.

Grasshopper listened with bated breath, and was even able to speak briefly with Harry during the break. His message at the podium: It was by no means certain that silver, then trading around $44 per ounce, was going to move above $50 again, or even hold its current price. Therefore, his recommendation was for investors to place a stop on existing positions at $37.50. If the price declined to this level, Harry believed the bullish case for higher values would be weakened enough to usher in a major decline, possibly marking an end to silver's epic bull market.

The air was electric. Here in person was the man who more than any other had influenced this acolyte's own thinking about silver and its investment value. In part it had led him to begin accumulating the metal at $4.23 an ounce several years before prices exploded, then adding more physical metal on the way up, with $38/ounce being the last and highest price paid. In the run from $10, he bought and sold futures contracts, taking large profit chunks out of a rapidly-ascending, seemingly unstoppable market run.

As an example of the volatility taking place, during one three day period, silver prices rocketed upward by $4.00 per ounce – for a long-side COMEX 5,000 ounce contract, that would represent an increase of $20,000!

Grasshopper originally intended to phone at the conference lunch break and call in a stop loss at $37.50 on all positions. So what happened?

Several other speakers that morning presented their opinions – all bullish in the extreme, and soon the temptation to hold on for higher prices took over. It's important to note here that this "don't sell factor" was not primarily one of greed. Rather it had to do with ignoring one's gut, ignoring salient input from the speaker who had been the top "cheerleader" for the metals during the entire bull market. It would later prove fully the truism that "If you don't sell when you can, you will surely sell when you must."

When you're given the answer but you can't believe it. Soon thereafter, the Canadian seer Jerome Smith, Harry Browne's former employer and the man who had literally "written the book" predicting $50 silver, rose to speak. He was now talking about his new target of $100 the ounce! Though not obvious at the time, it would shortly become vividly apparent that the psychological opportunity of stepping off the escalator with life-altering financial gains in order to beat the rush and leave the party early had been missed.

Not long afterwards, things began to go south as the silver market's internal structure started collapsing like bulkheads in the Titanic after being gored by an iceberg. The Powers at the COMEX, known today in some investor circles as the "CRIMEX", enforced a rule that silver futures contracts could only be sold, not purchased.

Shortly thereafter, the white metal's price cracked, in a few weeks disintegrating to a panic low of $10.80 per ounce. Grasshopper did some offsetting (sell orders) on the way down and kept significant profits, but a large equity portion years in the making, went up in smoke. Later as prices laboriously climbed back toward $25, significant additional profits returned to his futures account, but only with great effort.(Another caveat - prices tend to fall several times faster than they have risen!) The easy money days were over. In retrospect, the great gold and silver metal bull market had been mortally wounded. In spite of several "flash in the pan" rallies, it was going to be many brutal years before silver finally bottomed out below $5 an ounce.

Let this lesson of mine speak volumes to you. Do not get too greedy, listen to all; follow none. Years later, Harry Browne told me (David Morgan) he had not thought much about the timing on exiting the market. His editor did, and suggested to him that taking profits might be prudent.

Harry agreed, and was therefore one of the very few to get his "followers" out at the top. <u>The opportunity to make a call of this nature and its importance, for those who follow and listen to my work will be one of the primary drivers of my research and speaking engagements over the next few years, as this legendary bull market works its inevitable way toward the exits.</u>

The Old Lady talks to the Guru

On the last day of the San Francisco conference, this writer (David Smith) happened to enter a large speakers' hall, which was at the time completely deserted except for two people standing down near the front of the platform. One was an elderly, well-dressed lady. The other was Jerome Smith. Wishing to speak to the silver legend, but not wanting to interrupt the conversation, a respectful distance was kept, but it was obvious that she was seeking information on how to go about investing in silver. After they finished, we spoke for awhile. It would be fascinating to know if that lady went ahead and placed her funds into silver and gold, how much she might have invested, and how she fared thereafter. Especially so, given how close in time the metals were to breaking apart and beginning a generational bear market decline.

Reminiscences of a Stock Operator, penned by Edwin Lefevre – is widely believed to either be a pseudonym of the legendary speculator, Jesse Lauriston Livermore, the "Boy Plunger", or else was formulated in connection with a journalistic writing partnership. By any standard, it is one of the most insightful investment volumes ever written. *Reminiscences* is really a study in human nature, because as investors, the type of actions we take – and when we take them – are of critical significance to the end result.

Of the investing public, Livermore once said: "Play the market only when all factors are in your favor. No person can play the market all the time and win."

It's as though he is speaking to us today, when he said, *The big money in booms is always first made by the public – on paper… and on paper it remains.* This is such a compelling statement that we placed it on our book cover. It's message is a leitmotif of *Second Chance.* A cautionary remark that anyone reading this book ignores… at their peril.

Why does the public invariably make only <u>paper</u> profits? Because **not one person in ten thousand** has ever asked, let alone given thought to, a small set of crucial questions. Questions which MUST be answered ahead of time by each and every investor who has dreams of <u>keeping</u> a significant portion of his/her earnings once the evolving metals' mega-move draws to a close.

Why do I trade/How Much is enough (for Me)? The idea that you have enough money so you only have to work if/when you want, can be a powerful goal-setting motivation. It becomes sustainable once you've reached a sort of "critical mass", especially if you are able to keep expenditures below your level of income.

If your lifestyle ratchets up to "accommodate" the extra funding, it's not going to work. How much would you need to live like this? How much time/effort/risk are you willing to expend? Don't forget that even the time it takes is a cost. It takes "life-time" to make money. Can you dial back substantially – or all together – this expenditure over time? If you <u>could</u> live forever, would you really want to put up with indefinitely, on a full-time basis, the neuroses of the market's crowds?

Let a quote by Felix Dennis, one Britain's wealthiest men sink in. In his book *How to Get Rich*, he says *If you are young, you are infinitely richer than I can ever be again.*

It's worth taking a moment to reflect upon what Jim Rogers has to say about money management and how he goes about making it. Rogers drove around the world twice, once on a motorcycle and once in a car, and wrote a book about each trip. Admitting to being a poor market timer, he has nonetheless been willing to discuss how he does it. He just waits around for a situation that pretty much can't miss – where he metaphorically sees "money sitting in a corner". Then he goes over and picks it up..

Interviewed by John Train, he said you should**,**

> "take your money, put it in Treasury bills or a money-market fund. Just sit back, go to the beach, go to the movies, play checkers, do whatever you want to. Then something will come along where you know it's right. Take all your money out of the money-market fund, put it in whatever it happens to be, and stay with it for three or four or five or ten years, whatever it is. You'll know

when to sell again, because you'll know more about it than anybody else. Take your money out, put it back in the money-market fund, and wait for the next thing to come along. When it does, you'll make a whole lot of money."

Of course, in order to behave like this, you must have enough beyond daily needs so that you can earmark a portion for investment, and <u>then refrain from consuming this seed capital</u> while you watch for a "can't miss" opportunity.

It appears to be how legendary hedge fund founder, George Soros (with whom Jim Rogers used to work), planned for things during the weeks leading up to the 2016 "Brexit" vote that would ask UK citizens whether or not they wanted to remain in the European Union. It is reported that the 85 year-old Soros actually came out of retirement in order to personally place massive bets against possible outcomes as a result of the contest. Word is, that, as a result of the vote, he was able to locate quite a bit of money that was just "sitting in a corner."

As we've stated, the professionals strive to buy within twenty percent of a bottom. You can achieve this several ways. One is to begin your position by setting up a line with a series of orders to buy at Limit, good 'til cancelled (GTC), scale down into weakness. Then turn off the computer and go fishing, head to the golf course or spend time with the grandchildren. Waiting for that special moment seems to work for just about every informed, patient, highly-skilled investor/speculator on the globe. Most of the time they do nothing. But once they spy something special, it's ready, set, go!

IF you can make... and take... big money out of the coming metals' and miners' mania, it might be possible the next time an attractive opportunity presents itself, to invest just like Jim Rogers. And in the interim, spend as much time as he does, doing something else. Crocodiles, sharks and pythons don't search for 3 meals a day. One big score and they're fine for quite a while. Can an investor make and hold onto money the same way?

Brown Trout Investing

The German Brown Trout, arguably the most wary and finicky member of the trout family, is a master at paying attention to its surroundings. It takes up a feeding station and waits patiently for just the right morsel to drift down in front of it. It doesn't attack everything that happens by, but is extremely selective when it does. To give you an idea of just how selective - on a particular river in Patagonia, in a run of 90,000 Sea Trout (sea-run browns) less than 10% ever take an angler's offering, and probably less than one quarter of those are landed.

Consider imitating a Brown Trout! If the water temperature is not to their liking, they don't bite. If it's too sunny, they sit on the bottom in deep water. If a fly isn't the right size, color and swing - no dice. If they do take a fly, and get a sense that it's not real, they spit it out (cut their loss). They would almost rather feed at night than during the day - try catching one after dark when you can't see which way it's running -upstream or down!

Wait for a "can't lose trade." Be selective of which mining stock or ETP you buy. Don't attempt to get a full meal with one trade - take and offset your position "one bite at a time." Be willing to wait a long time before you "strike."

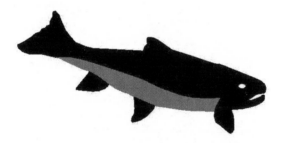

Big Trout (courtesy Steven A. Smith)

More than Making Money: Living, Fishing, and Investing the Jim Teeny Way

As the frenetic pace of life in today's Internet-driven world continues to accelerate, where things can shift before you've even finished reading an article dealing with change, it's easy to forget about the behaviors and values that give our lives purpose and special meaning. Maybe it's time to step back a bit and see how someone else is doing it. You could, we suppose, follow the example of Henry Ford. When asked the question, "How much is enough?" He is said to have replied..."Just a little bit more."

We <u>can</u> guarantee that if you begin take stock of your thinking and behavior now, along with the effort to plan and execute a trading program, your journey to the precious metals bull market top will be enriched immeasurably in more ways than you might think.

You might take a page from Jim Teeny's playbook. Since 1962, when Jim's late father suggested that he might catch more fish on an "ugly" fly than a pretty one, he has been tying what has become in the fly fishing world, an iconic pattern - the Teeny Nymph. Jim's fly pattern has held over 30 International Game Fish Association (IGFA) World Records, and as he notes, "We've probably released another thirty-five or forty fish (species) in addition, just because we didn't want to harm them."

Can we learn something from Jim's behavior that applies to the world of investment? (Listen to a short interview *here* (or you can go to vimeo. com and search for "The Legend - Jim Teeny" and decide for yourself.)

And he's done all of this with a Ring-necked Pheasant 3 variation pattern, tied using 13 colors of tail feathers and a dozen hook sizes. For inventing and popularizing this "simple" pattern, Jim's template Teeny Nymph was featured as "The Fly of the Year for Oregon" at the 2014 Federation of Fly Fishers Conference in Albany.

In fishing and investing - look for the "real deal"

Whether stalking fish, precious metals, or mining stocks, "go where the big ones are known to be." - Jim targets streams and lakes in various locales around the world that have proven over time to hold large numbers of big trout, salmon, bonefish or tarpon, offering him a good return on the time and money spent.

Purchase your silver, gold and palladium from a trusted source who honors their word with a history of strong customer service. You might rightfully hesitate traveling to a remote fishing spot based upon a third-hand rumor, without more substantial evidence from someone reliable who's actually been there. To protect yourself, strive to buy precious metals the same way. (The majority of this segment was published in 2015 at moneymetals.com where this writer -David Smith - writes a monthly column. He does not receive remuneration for anyone who might be inclined to become one of their customers.)

Teeny Nymphs and 1/10th troy oz. Silvers
(courtesy Jim Teeny and Money Metals Exchange)

Get your gear ready <u>before</u> the run gets underway

Migratory salmon and trout are only found in their native rivers at certain times during the year. If you're too early, you may end up working an empty stream and go home skunked.

With precious metals, "being early" simply means that you're likely to get a much better price than if you waited until "the run is on." Stack your coins ahead of time, then relax and enjoy the trend while others are fretting about how and where they're going to get theirs.

You're much better off being quite a bit early... than a day or a week too late!

The same goes for setting up a mining position. When your analysis, using a variety of technical tools, indicates a company is on the uptrend, start laying in your position in tranches, preferably on reactions against the primary trend. If you've identified a particular stock as a core holding, resist the urge to trade it out until you believe the majority of the move upside has ended.

Valid principles work time after time...

Jim closes one of his instructional videos by saying, "The Teeny Nymph has worked for me for forty-one years, and I'm telling you, that you're going to do just as good as I am on this pattern. Give it a try."

For several thousand years and across cultures, people have chosen silver (and gold) as insurance - as real money - and nowadays, especially in the case of silver - as "health insurance" for medicinal purposes and in over 10,000 industrial applications.

Have confidence in your stock analysis. After you've gone through the OODA Loop, perhaps more than once - be sure to act on the plan you've put together. Once you've learned and applied valid trading principles, they will continue to work, time after time.

You can do Good <u>and</u> Well:

Inspired by Donna Teeny, Jim at jimteeny.com offers products specifically designed for *Casting for Recovery*, a non-profit educational program for women surviving breast cancer, and *Project Healing Waters*, a non-profit organization teaching fly fishing and fly tying skills to American servicemen and women.

As a metals and mining stock investor, you have the opportunity to operate from a multi-dimensional perspective - doing both good and well. Give a tip, a gift, or help someone on the street? When an opportunity presents itself, rather than offering "paper promises" - a term coined by David Morgan, donate a small amount of real money, which unlike every form of paper currency ever issued, has **never** seen its value fall to zero! Place a one-tenth ounce .999 fine silver round in someone's palm - and watch their eyes light up!

We've done it on our trips to South American countries - to cab drivers, waiters, fishing guides, and lodge operators. When you give someone who has just experienced a 25% devaluation of their currency even a small amount of silver, you can be sure you've got their attention!

Whether it's fly fishing, buying precious metals, or some other activity you decide to pursue, it doesn't have to be complicated. It isn't necessary to make a huge leap in perspective or practice in order to succeed for yourself while helping others. Being grateful for what you have - as well as what you might be able to earn through your investing efforts will keep you humble and centered. Most of us know in our hearts what's right. If you're not satisfied with how things are flowing right now - whether it involves fishing or investing - chances are the way you're going about it will only involve a "Teeny" change!

Decide <u>now</u> how much is enough

Is your answer to this question "Just a little bit more!"? Or is it more nuanced and limited? Either way, you need to find out – well before the market is peaking and your emotions have become captive to the public's hysteria. If you wait, we'd guess the odds you'll get around to thinking about it are going to be quite low... similar to your trading account balance after the precious metals' market top has come and gone.

Look deep inside, and ask why you want to spend the time, money and energy in this market. Talk to friends and associates who lost tens, hundreds of thousands, or millions of dollars in 2000 as one of the greatest stock market bubbles in history disintegrated. Would having some kind of plan to "get out early" with a portion of their winnings have made a difference for those who did not? We'd answer in the affirmative, and we'll seek to demonstrate just that.

In spite of recent nominal stock market highs, calculate the math, and back out the inflation rate for the last 16 years, and you'll find that the Dow/S&P500 are close to flat in inflation-adjusted terms. Secular stock bulls and bears tend to last around 16-18 years each. So odds are good that the bear market which began in 2000 has yet to fully wring out the excess of the preceding phase. Could it be in line for another visit towards Dow 6600 within the next couple of years?

Many – we know of them or were in this situation ourselves – were emotionally unable to open their 401k statements in order to see what had been done to trading balances, retirement accounts, college programs, (fill in the blank). Years of effort, investment, and ego attachment gone up in smoke. A nine year decline, then another seven years to break even or slightly more. There must be a better way.

AGQ 2011-15, note reverse splits (courtesy Stockcharts.com)

As earlier stated, ETFs seldom make a good choice as a core holding or a long term position trade. Mental or actual stop-loss protection is highly recommended. The following weekly chart of AGQ, the ProShares Ultra Silver provides visual proof. After the 2011 break it traded from over 350/share, down to 180, declined to the point where it underwent a 1:2 split, then continued on down to $20/share. The same fate of reverse splits can befall an ETF trading below $5.

Investors <u>selling</u> 500 million ounces of silver?

In 2015 alone Investors in the U.S. purchased 100 million ounces of physical silver. Multiply that by several years going forward. It's a good bet that as we get into long-term topping action, a fair amount of that metal is going to come back into the market, looking for a home. How much and to what effect? We don't have an opinion just now, but not keeping track of such a trend if/as it develops, let alone ignoring it all together, might not be the most sensible strategy.

Decide **now** that at some point, you will take a profit and not worry that you missed the exact top. There is no more devastating investment activity than watching a position you have spent years acquiring, being ground to bits as the market relentlessly moves against you. But that's exactly what does (and will) happen when an aging bull market hands off the baton to a long-term secular bear. If you're still fully invested when the Big Change gets underway, your portfolio will eventually look like a piñata that's had a machete taken to it. And it may one day be worth about as much...

In the end, after making and losing several fortunes, Livermore took his own life by putting a gun to his head in a public restroom. Though he may have been a victim of what we now call bipolar disorder, we wonder if he ever reflected upon the key question that everyone reading this text should identify and resolve for themselves. How much is enough?

In *Reminiscences*, he remarked "A loss never bothers me after I take it – but being wrong – not taking the loss – is what damages pocket and soul." Is it a given, that investors are destined to take that big loss, after an epic run where many things were done right, earning profits beyond one's wildest expectations? Doing all of this, only to see a portfolio slashed to ribbons? Considerable evidence points to a conclusion that a fundamental misunderstanding of the markets, of human nature, and of themselves leads them by their actions - or inactions- inevitably to such a dark corner.

The Internet's Double-Edged Trading Sword:

Many people reading this have no experience with investing as it existed 20 or 30 years ago. Before the Internet. When sending attachments, company reports, Brokerage newsletters and "Special Situation" analyses by what we now call "snail mail" was the rule, rather than the exception. When you called up your broker to make a trade and read the order on the phone. When there were no ETFs, but rather mutual funds. You placed a buy or sell order by 12 noon, then waited a few hours to see what the settlement prices was - after the market's close, when the net asset value (NAV) of the fund had been computed for the day.

Yes, the big brokerage houses still have an edge, use high frequency trading, bet against their clients, use their clients' money to gamble, and invest in "dark pools" with off-exchange quotes that offer better, quicker fills than you and I get when we trade.

But *we* also have the analytical tools to call up a company's website, look at their data, including company presentations, speak with management, and then make a trade at a discount broker for $5 - $10 a side, rather than $65 in the old days. There's a fair amount of junk in the newsletter business, as has always been the case. But there are outstanding letters out there as well (Including of course, *The Morgan Report*!), several of which we've gone out of our way to profile in this book, without expectation of remuneration for doing so.

Primitives with Computers

In short, ALMOST everything in our trading environment has changed, and will continue to do so, while at the same time humans are still making decisions from their reptilian brain. We're "primitives with computers." When our portfolio positions "come under attack" the tendency is to respond just like we would on the street against an assault. Fight, Flee or Freeze. And now we can make emotional, ill-thought out decisions... from a smart phone!

In the '70s or '80s, it might have taken quite awhile for a major top to form; these days it can happen in a heartbeat. A quote from an article at time.com/money by Penelope Wang illustrates the change. Citing research from Duke University, the study notes that on financial literacy tests, people scored considerably worse on mobile devices than they did when using pen and paper.

> "One possible reason is that you might think and act faster in front of screens, which leads to a greater reliance on instinctive responses that are often incorrect. At the same time, mobile devices tend to make you more impulsive. This research suggests that a lot of important financial transactions, like taking money out of your 401(k), should probably not happen on mobile."

A Caltech study on market behavior offers evidence that faster communication offers a bigger downside to those who have not fully formed their decision-making processes, saying that,

> "The risks of herding behavior may be even greater today. In the last crash, social media was just getting going. Now, with market moves triggering alerts on smart phones worldwide, the next market plunge may be led by a social media panic. When millions of people see their balances shrink on their devices, and they are being urged to act quickly, and they can, it's likely to make the next crash much worse."

All the more reason to get your planning and thinking down now, well before the markets really heat up. Practice the OODA Loop. Your trading ace in the hole.

What is <u>My</u> Exit Strategy?

When making an investment, people generally think only about where to buy, without much consideration about when, how, or even *if* they might sell. But, as you must have guessed by now, our idea is to set things up so as to be able to make <u>and keep</u> a substantial profit. What are the approaches an astute trader might take, as down the line this great gold and silver bull market grows to maturity and eventually comes to an end?

CHAPTER 9

Leave the Wave:
Part I Why and How

*When it comes, it bears the grim face of disaster. That is because both of the groups of participants in the speculative situation are programmed for sudden efforts at escape. Something — it matters little-although it will always be much debated — triggers the ultimate reversal. Those who had been riding the upward wave decided now is the time to get out. Those who thought the increase would be forever find their illusion destroyed abruptly, and they, also, respond to the newly revealed reality by selling or trying to sell. Thus the collapse. And thus the rule, supported by the experience of centuries: the speculative episode always ends not with a whimper but with a bang." - **John Kenneth Galbraith***

During the final phase, this precious metals' mega-bull market will continue rising - just like the 2000 dotcom bull did - until it has humbled ALL naysayers. We remember that when Sir John Templeton announced he was going short 100 stocks, some "reporters" spoke derisively about how he was getting well up in years (implying senility). He just wasn't with the times. Sir John was too critical of a market that had returned an average of 24% for each of the preceding four years... and which was certainly going to continue at that pace for the foreseeable future...

During the frenzied march to the ultimate top, it will be difficult for any market participant who still has a position, to "stay long and strong." And it will be dangerous. Dangerous because the desire to keep a position - and presumably keep making money - will seduce all but the most focused, self-disciplined individuals to hold on longer for the possibility of still bigger - seemingly endless profits.

Technical indicators, economic reports, market sentiment, everything... will be "indicating" that the market *must* continue to move higher. Possibly the only thing that flashes a warning will be your gut, or your experience in other markets. But without some kind of plan that not only fits your financial goals, investment capital levels - but most importantly your temperament - you're almost certainly going to act/react impulsively to what's going on in the increasingly emotionally-elevated atmosphere of the marketplace.

Ultimately this will lead, as all market mania tops have before, to the majority of its participants overstaying their welcome. Often, a major top puts in an initial devastating smash; recoups 50% of the previous drop, consolidates for awhile, then rolls over and heads down for the count... for a long, long time.

In early 1980, Silver hit $50 an ounce. A couple of months later, it broke down from the $37 dollar level and over the next few days, and plummeted to an initial collapse level of $10.80. After several months more, it rose to touch the $25 level (the classic 50% retracement!) We asked our broker at the time where he thought silver would ultimately end up (down). His answer - "It will go to $5." It eventually dropped to around $4.35.

A long time for a bull to hold on to an investment that had now become a secular bear. Sitting through a number of false metal rallies that after awhile, turned out to be nothing more than cyclical bull markets within the context of the much more pervasive and longer-lasting downtrend. A long, corrosive wait of many years - decades -for the next gold and silver bull market to get underway.

We believe there is a reliable way to "hang in there" well into the inevitable topping process, and get out with the majority of one's accumulated profits. It can work for you because the philosophy behind it addresses, not only the critical concept of risk/reward analysis, but also enables you to temper what some call the "twin dragons" of the market place - fear and greed. It can keep you from riding like many did, the exploration stock mentioned earlier - from .35 cents to $10.00 to .11 cents a share, and either selling out as its perceived value headed towards a dime, or holding on through inertia, and picking up a few crumbs when it was taken out at .80 cents.

"De-Risking" your core portfolio into the last few innings

Before we get there, let's look at some strategies which might enable you to take serious "profit vitamins" out of the bull trend, so that more and more, you're placing less and less of your original financial stake at risk. Like in a Las Vegas gambling casino, you're sweeping some winning chips off the table, relying more on the House money to fund your continued involvement in the Big Gamble. Done this way, for you, it can become more of a finely calculated risk.

Exit Strategy #1: The Sandwich Trader

One way to make a significant profit and still get out in time is to become a "Sandwich Trader." Initiate a position well after a perceived new trend has begun, with the intention of holding on for a portion of the ride and taking a good-sized chunk from the center. The decision is usually made after consulting charts to identify a bottoming formation, such as a spike low, a higher low/higher high pattern, or what appears to be a double – even a triple bottom. Confirmation comes from seeing volume increase when the price rises, and decrease as it falls. And of course, the old lows should hold. All of this taken together indicates to the sandwich trader that a new, substantive trend has probably begun.

If the commodity or stock in question has fallen, say 80% beforehand over an extended period – but analysis builds a case that the long term "value proposition" is still compelling, then the possibility of outsized gains is greatly enhanced for the patient investor who quietly builds a position when most peoples' attention is focused elsewhere.

What's intriguing about mining stocks in general and silver in particular, is that we are now being presented with this very condition. Across the board, junior producers have seen share prices decline by this magnitude, even as they have increased production, cut operating costs and in many cases added significantly to their resource base, assuring additional years of high quality resource for their milling operations.

Using this example as a guideline, a Sandwich Trader (ST) would have watched the metals and miners during the 4th quarter of 2015, and noted the rounded bottoming patterns of gold and silver in December. He/she would have paid particular attention to the false breakdown in many miners on January 19, 2016, and become quite interested in gold's response to challenging and finding support at the $1,200 level after it tried to hit $1,300. Positions might have been established when $1,200 held, and by late April/early May, this kind of trader would have established core positions, which could be held until gold/silver either broke out convincingly above their 2011 highs, or attempted and failed to do so over several months.

A more conservative Sandwich Trader might wait for what they perceived to be an "all-clear" with a convincing gold base built above the round number of $1,500, and above $26 silver. Note how much "potential profit" this kind of trader did NOT access during the extraordinary January - late summer period of that year. But this observation is not the point. The concept is that an ST is primarily interested in taking a big bite out of the middle of a perceived intermediate to long term move, while mitigating risk.

During the infamous 2008 – 2015 period, silver twice lost 60% of its value, fully earning its sobriquet "the restless metal". All the reasons silver began its rise from the $4 level soon after the new century began are not only still valid, but arguably even more compelling than before. The upside potential for the investor who employs such a strategy, and the relative risk- for the person who simply seeks to "take a bite out of the middle" - is truly breath-taking.

The Sandwich Trader (ST) Says "Good-bye"

Like a whale filtering clouds of krill through its baleen, the ST, taking a big bite out of the middle, exits weighed down with profits, well before the party is over. This type of trader easily layers out as the market, which at that point consists of many new recruits in addition to a legion of longer term true believers, gladly accepts the ST's positions he/she so carefully acquired before the potential was fully recognized. The risk of a major give-back of the ST's profits is almost zero. It's close to a sure thing that both the entry and exit will go completely unnoticed.

Why don't more of us behave this way? Because the universal trait is an even greater dread of missing out on larger profits by leaving early, as contrasted with the fear of losing what has already been earned.

In an interview conducted while this book was being written, I (David Morgan) made the following comments about how unusual this kind of trading is, in relation to the mindset and approach most investors (who are generally unsuccessful) take, saying,

> "The problem with a lot of people is that they have an amateur's perspective - which means they think that if they didn't get in at the low, they've missed the move. Actually the best traders and the wealthiest people on the planet just take out the middle. In other words they may not even get into the market again until it's past $26 (At the time I made this statement, silver was trading below $21.), then ride it from 26 to 46, get out and take massive amounts of money from the market as silver goes up to a hundred. They know what they're doing; they're not trading in hindsight."

The only way to contain this anxiety is to decide beforehand, then follow through <u>decisively</u> when the time and exit target zones have arrived. Once you depart, thoroughly disassociate yourself – and your image from that investment. And never look back.

A Canadian ST who bought silver at $11, sold at $18, and made millions.

Prior to the 1980 top in silver, this writer knew a very successful Canadian trader who operated exactly in this fashion. Though he wrote a book about his system, and for awhile had a newsletter outlining his tactics, he was - and still is - virtually unknown to the general public, even to most professional traders.

Using proprietary technical analysis, some of which has since found its way onto public trading platforms, he waited patiently –often YEARS, for a given market to meet his criteria of having formed a major bottom. After determining a series of entry points, he began to establish a large position. Acting upon his trading signals, he sold lightly into major resistance, then added more into deep reactions against the new trend. Along the way, he continually monitored his indicators, keeping an eye out for evidence that the risk-reward ratio was shifting in a way that might invalidate his original premise. He looked for a change in the market's tone that would cause him to exit completely and permanently, thus concluding that investment campaign.

When the profile of a commodity he held changed, calling into question his original premise, he would without hesitation offset 100%. For good. He literally burned his charts. Although this is a sound strategy, very few people can actually do it. If you are to become financially independent, acquiring the financial freedom of doing what you wish with your time, you absolutely must have a plan of some sort. So start thinking ahead of time as to what you will do if your profits become sufficient for allowing you to walk away.

Sometimes "the Canadian" left a lot of money on the table. During the 1978-80 silver run, he bought at $11 and ended his campaign around $18. Even when silver rose to $50, he didn't complain, make excuses, or try to get back in. He also didn't lose a penny when silver later collapsed back down to $10, on its way to $5.

This one silver campaign earned him millions in profit. Could *you* make a trade like this, then watch (or ignore!) with aplomb as the price where you sold it almost tripled thereafter? A good Sandwich Trader - in this case an epic one - is capable of doing just that.

Now, consider this. Do you believe it's possible to stay in the game on a move of the magnitude which silver offered investors in the 1980 run up, and which may once again become available – this time around with a profit potential several times greater than before?

If you're willing to accept a pre-determined risk with a portion of your trading account, and have previously worked out a focused, clearly-stated plan, then a strong - no - a compelling case can be made that you have a shot at the extraordinary amount of additional profits which a sandwich trader, by dint of his investment principles, leaves on the table. As we will shortly demonstrate, this bears no relationship to selling out, then attempting to get back in after a big break.

Exit Strategy #2: Laddering Out

A number of tools exist for measuring the duration/distance of a price move. Some, like the Finger Spread, are low tech. Black Box programs reputed to divine the future are available for as much as a trader is willing to spend. But given the track record of these systems (always 'back-tested'), it might be better to toss Oracle bones while consulting the *I-Ching*.

An approach which doesn't involve the use of advanced calculations was detailed a number of years ago by Arthur Skarlew. His *Techniques of a Professional Commodity Chart Analyst,* now most likely out of print, offers effective and easily understandable ways to set targets.

His "Rule of 7" is particularly interesting. Over the years, it has divined an impressive number of accurate target areas for a variety of investment vehicles. Indeed, Sandwich Traders could find it to be a priceless addition to their investment tool kit. Keeping things simple, all the math can be performed with a calculator or paper and pencil. After you've chosen your targets, place (GTC) sell stops around those points, or "set" them mentally. Once you've taken a position, understand that you become part of the crowd.

A second trading book that may interest readers who want to delve deeply into TA is *Come into My Trading Room*, by Dr. Alexander Elder. A devotee will find much of interest therein.

Selling into strength; Buying back into a reaction

Another effective way to lock in profits, is to sell tranches, scale up into a strongly rising trend. Just the opposite of scaling down, you attempt to take as much profit as possible when the price is moving in your favor. If you're following the "buy and sell less than is rational" approach when you start to make a trade, and start to feel yourself getting swept up in the market's emotions... cut the size of your order by 25 - 50%.

As long as the primary trend remains up, and prices are falling into a reaction, you goal is to buy one or more tranches at progressively lower levels – decreasing your average cost in preparation for the next leg. In a dynamic market like 2016, you may only get one chance per decline to add.

When the primary trend changes, so must traders change in order to survive. Since the market does not "ring a bell at the top" few investors will initially understand that something fundamentally different has taken place. For awhile, the more adroit and lucky ones will make money, but before long, many still in the market will have gone flat broke because of "averaging down" - which only works when the primary trend is up. Many more will be destined to watch their stock balance erode away, month after month after year, until they can't take it anymore, and close their accounts. Or until they just stop opening their monthly brokerage statements.

Jim Sinclair says that mining shares tend to behave in a certain way during a precious metals' bull market cycle: "Early and late in the market, the juniors perform well; in the middle it's 'bow wow' for the juniors." Right about now you will almost certainly look into the future and assume that these stocks might – in a best case scenario - rise only somewhat above their 2006/2011 highs. And you might be wrong.

Don't have "too small a picture"

History is replete with examples of politicians and generals who - because their picture was not big enough -forfeited an unexpected opportunity to magnify a newly-achieved success by ten or a hundred times. Had the Japanese Imperial Navy not turned around before entering Leyte Gulf, they most likely would have destroyed an unprotected Allied troop fleet at anchor (The war would not have ended differently, but the U.S. might have been dealt one of its most devastating wartime losses.) A Syrian general (later executed) during a middle east war, couldn't believe that a central highway bisecting Israel could possibly be undefended, so he hesitated overnight, and lost his chance to change history; An American Colonial army did not press its advantage during an attempted invasion of eastern Canada - which might have brought our northern neighbor under the control of the new nation to the south.

Cornwallis at Yorktown, not realizing that by holding out for a few more days, he would have been relieved by a British fleet laden with soldiers sailing toward his position, lost a continent; The Inca Chief Atahualpa, allowing a few dozen Conquistadors to rout his personal bodyguard using unfamiliar weaponry... forfeited an empire. Hitler first allowed the British Expeditionary Force (BEF) to escape by sea from Dunkirk. Then during the ensuing weeks, while the British Aisles were essentially defenseless, he would not gamble on an airborne assault - losing the very real possibility of driving Britain to defeat and becoming the master of Europe.

Be sure you don't make an "historical" mistake with your trading account. Don't limit your "picture" about how high these stocks can go based upon the 2000-2016 record. If you sell out that position way too soon – it might still go up another 10x as the public piles in while you watch from the sidelines! Keep in mind the old saw that's heard in Vancouver mining finance circles about being in on the action when an investment opportunity goes down.

"If you're out of the room, you're out of the deal!"

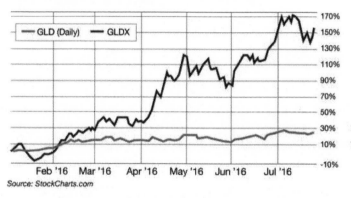

Source: StockCharts.com

Gold (GLD) vs. Gold Companies (GLDX)

On July 19, 2016, was published what we believe to have been a very important article, with special relevance for mining stock traders/investors. If the author's perspective turns out to be correct, it should bring to bear considerable psychological support to both our thesis and your efforts. *The Chartology of a Generational Precious Metals Miner Move,* was posted at rambus1.com (not to be confused with semiconductor, memory systems and IP products producer, Rambus Inc.) You may be able to find a more detailed description of this report in the public domain using a search engine.

Rambus' chart, looking at the GOLD:$XAU ratio, indicates that after 20 years of physical gold price outperformance relative to the mining stocks, the relationship may now have changed, with the miners outperforming gold, both in relative terms, and at the relative speed with which the miners' rise *vis á vis* gold is taking place. He says:

> "We are witnessing an unprecedented rebalancing of the precious metals' stocks to gold. This started in January of this year and shows no signs of abating. If you've been a precious metals' investor... this is the absolute best buying opportunity in 20 years to buy your favorite precious metals' stocks. The unwinding of the parabolic 20 year arc is something you don't see every day, and to be on the ground floor of the rebalancing move should be very rewarding if one can stay in the saddle.... This is a very interesting setup we have in the precious metals stocks right now that few understand the magnitude of what may lie ahead."

And finally:

> "One either believes we are in a new bull market in the PM complex or they don't. There are never any guarantees when it comes to the markets but one has to trade on what they see based on their charts or whatever trading discipline you use to make a judgment call. I firmly believe that the bear market in the PM complex ended on January 19th of 2016 and a new bull market, within the secular bull market, has begun that could last for years into the future..."

While being detailed, Rambus' on-site analysis is crisp, clear and tightly stated. Few in the newsletter industry meet our high standards, but from what we have seen, rambus1.com operates at a similar level as our own *Morgan Report*.

Near the top, this *could* happen to a stock - and to you.

What follows in rounded dollars is an example of a real-life mining stock whose name for the purpose of this discussion is not important – but the concept it illustrates is everything. Looking just at the largest swings over 18 years, in 1996 it traded at $4/share. In 2001, its low was a bit under $3; 2004 had a high of $18; 2008 had a high of $40 and a low of $12. In 2010, the high was c. $41. It's 2015 low was $5.85. Thus it has twice exceeded $41.

IF this particular stock still has what it takes, and IF our premise is correct that an historic precious metals' blow-off phase still lies ahead, the following COULD happen to any number of mining stocks, at some point during the next few years.

Over time, this stock rises from its current depressed state and manages to print new all time highs above $40/share. You, having bravely held through these swings since 2002, are overjoyed, and sell portions at $50, $60 and $70, with your last offset at $75. Because you've made a really nice score and are considered by all of your friends and neighbors to be a mining stock-picking guru, you buy all of them two rounds of drinks at the local bar.

Shortly thereafter, two things have taken place. First, the beers you've had drinking are beginning to wear off. Second, you no longer have a position in this stock. Two months later it prints a price of $225 a share.

You did everything right, got out of your position into strength, and made a lot of money. But, with a small portion of your account, you could have done one thing differently. By accepting a predetermined $ risk, you could have held on to some of your position. Of course, where you sold at $75 might have been the top. But here's the thing... it was not. You missed another 300% of potential profit because you failed to develop and utilize the type of portfolio tool we're going to discuss shortly...

In a few years, near the end of our historic bull run saga, volatility – in both directions –will be off the charts. If the 1980 experience is any guide, the mining sector top may take place months after the metals themselves print their top mark, but we can only guess about that ahead of time. A factor influencing the outcome will have to do with the availability of physical gold and silver in relation to demand. If metal cannot be supplied in sufficient quantity, and demand continues to be robust, it's reasonable to expect that the demand overflow will find its way into "metals' substitutes" – the mining stocks. Either way, dozens if not scores of miners, and ETFs, <u>hold the potential</u> of behaving the same way as the $4 - $225 mining stock scenario just discussed.

A background question to what we've talked about is this: "Assuming you somehow stayed long on this stock, are you now willing to ride it down again, to say...$35? We didn't think so. Our portfolio approach is going to give you some serious coverage on that issue as well.

Exit Strategy #3: Listen to Your Gut.

Primitive man was more attuned to his surroundings than most of us are today. Their vision may not have been better, their brain was probably smaller, but no doubt smell, taste and hearing were highly evolved and the signals received to their brain of whatever size were acted upon quickly - or not. A left-over specialty from that era is what we call "gut feel."

We've all had this sensation at one time or another, though we seldom act on it. Instead we seek an intellectual explanation for what our stomach is trying to tell us. Being visual and cerebral creatures, we look for additional confirmation from our eyes and brain.

If you reflect on the number of times you've received these abdominal impulses and how often you've ignored the signals, you might be surprised. It's easy to overlook the feeling and go about your day. We'd suggest you should <u>always</u> pay attention to this helpful sensation. Brain mapping research has indicated that not only does the stomach have a similar communication setup to the brain, but it actually sends *more* signals to the brain than it receives! To the tune of 60%/40%, advantage stomach.

In early 2014, Dr. Joe Dispenza published a book titled, *You Are the Placebo*. As the follow-on work to an earlier book, *Breaking the Habit of Being Yourself,* he presents a compelling case that by realigning how we think, our future can be changed. Since we keep responding to new events in the same well-worn, unproductive ways, drawing on deeply-conditioned beliefs and emotions, repetitive unproductive outcomes are virtually assured.

A habituated thought, if not interrupted and changed, becomes a feeling. The body starts producing chemicals in support of it. The feeling develops into an emotion, and if produced often enough, along with other thoughts/habits, the sum total is an evolution into a temperament and finally a personality. Dr. Joe demonstrates convincingly that this behavior can be altered, calling on our newly-enhanced understanding of the brain's neuro-plasticity – its ability to create new communicative passageways, enabling altered habits and behaviors. By changing our response to a stimulus, we can sidestep our present response, and thereby set in motion behavioral patterns which can literally and fundamentally change our future.

What if you could change your response when the market is going against your position, so that you react differently than most other participants, becoming a more productive investor? Since everything we decide to do – be it a trade in the markets, planning for a vacation or mowing the lawn – begins with a thought, ponder this: If you tend to add to your positions after the market has risen, and sell out on big declines – the exact behaviors which leads to market losses -consider stopping the chain of events as soon as you begin feeling the urge to do so.

"Release" the thought before the brain calls up emotions, leading to the formulation of physical symptoms... before you "become emotional". Then before (instead of?) you can act on this feeling, replace it with something along the lines of,

"I release my formerly-destructive trading habits. Henceforth, I intend to sell only into price strength and buy only into weakness. I will always buy and sell 'less than is rational'."

By reprogramming yourself to behave in exactly the opposite way that most investors do – your investing future begins to change. Your trading decisions start to flow. You'll start to see yourself watching what's going on, rather than getting caught up as the market swings to and from its emotional extremes. This trait will be crucial if you intend to successfully navigate the rip-tide energies of a precious metals' bull market topping process.

You'll also become and remain healthier. Less cortisol because you're no longer so stressed out; clearer thinking because you're getting enough oxygen; less muscle pain due to a more relaxed physical posture - and more successful trading results, since you're no longer "running with the bulls" (or bears, as the case may be!). Over time you'll find yourself selling when others are buying, and buying when the crowds are selling. Just the opposite of what most investors do. Exactly the way "big names" in the trading arena act.

At the present time, it's safe to say that *You Are the Placebo* is not generally viewed as a work that can help a person realign their investment results. However, after having read both texts, and applying Dr. Joe's protocol to generate a variety of improved outcomes – not least in the investment arena, this writer suggests that you might want to give this title a serious look.

At the very least, when you get a "gut feel" about your market position, become hyper-vigilant until the reason or lack thereof for such awareness becomes apparent. Then make the proper response. Many traders set rules on money management, yet when they know in their gut that it is time to take the loss, or a gain, they ignore the feeling because for some reason, their own head (thinking) justifies breaking their own rule.

Just don't expect a print-out from Mr. Market right away. He's prone to manifesting a price point first, and explaining it later.

Exit Strategy # 4: "Enough" (For Your Own Good)

It's an article of faith by astute market observers that over time "prices revert to the mean." This has been true of soybeans, Tulip bulbs, real estate, and eventually it will be so for gold and silver. One of the variables gets out of whack, and prices either crater or explode to the upside. While the resulting unbalanced situation can last for quite awhile, prices invariably move back toward a balance. Especially after a move of many years in one direction, the price not only reverts to the mean, it overshoots in the opposite direction…just about always.

Looking at the histories of many traders both famous and unknown, this also seems to be the case in regard to their trading success and account balance. If you stay in the game long enough, "Mr. Market" will take back just about all you ever made.

Commodity trading records spanning decades show that almost no one can keep an "active lifestyle" in the markets and not be staggered to the mat sooner or later. Remember the Turtles and their famous trading leader from Chicago? No, not in reference to the 60's singing group of the same name! – although, one of their songs, loosely paraphrased, may have been on the mark for the purpose of our discussion - "I can't see me loving (trading) nobody but you (precious metals) for all my life."

There are rare exceptions. In the 1970's, two brothers no one had ever heard of opened a small commodities account. They caught swing moves in silver (in the days when the metal only moved a dollar or so per year) turning their $10,000 grubstake into $200,000 (worth over $1 million today). After a few months, they closed their account and disappeared.

Today, several "masters of the universe" trading houses, financed with "bail in" funds from taxpayers via our kleptocratic governmental distribution system, have made inordinate profits. High Frequency Trading (HFT) platforms generate well over half the general stock market's daily volume. "Regulatory" authorities, supposedly protecting the public, actually empower those whom they watch over ("regulatory capture"), with the result that those who play both sides make even more money and accrue more power - with the public losing out as per usual. If things go really wrong, the Fed steps in and infuses their operations with new money from the public purse, allowing the miscreants to leverage their trades even more.

Now, we're staring at negative interest rates, where the customer pays the bank for the privilege of keeping a cash balance in their own account. In Europe, trillions of dollars (euros) in long term bonds have been issued at negative rates.

It may seem that this kind of dysfunctional behavior can go on forever. Silver and gold make a solid run to the upside and are "capped" by large entities short-selling into them. The price collapses, the shorts are offset at big profits and new longs placed on to profit from the next rally. Time after time the public funds are relieved of their money by these manipulations – with no end in sight.

But consider one of the best known resource brokers, Rick Rule's observation: "Your expectations for the future are conditioned by your experiences in the immediate past. The market is bigger than the morons who are trying to suppress it."

Mr. Market is nothing, if not a measuring system, and sooner or later it *will* balance things out – perhaps nowhere more profoundly than in the silver market. If you are still onboard with even a relatively small position when that happens, your account balance could end up looking very promising indeed. (A more cerebral friend than this writer once remarked, "The wheels of justice grind slowly, but they grind fine.")

Know what you want, elevate your expectations, yet do not go for the ultimate high "tick". When silver and gold are talked about every day in the mainstream financial press, when gold is featured on the cover of Time magazine, when the Wall Street Journal recommends it, then please KNOW the time has come to lighten up if not get out completely!

Exit Strategy #5: When a significant other says "Honey, maybe you should sell."

This might fall under the category of a tactic, rather than market strategy, but it has put extra money in the pockets of more than a few investors. Or cost them a chunk of change when they ignored it! Before dismissing this suggestion out of hand, reflect for a moment. Here's an easy bet of a tube of 20 American Silver Eagles the odds are good, that after you have gone on at length about how much "profit" you accumulated on a certain trade, you've had a wife, relative or friend makes a comment. Over the years, it's happened to this writer several times - a soft voice of reason coming from someone who wouldn't know a Sacagawea dollar from a Krugerrand!

The phrase "Maybe you should sell", when uttered by an "amateur" (you're the pro, right?) - generally a female observer - more often than not marks the EXACT point <u>and</u> time of a market top of intermediate to long-term duration.

Exit Strategy #6: Doug the (West Coast) Barber

Some of the best investors are never written about in trade magazines, aren't seen on CNN, don't make the Financial Section, and are known of only by word of mouth. One of these is a man we'll call "Doug the Barber." Not only is he a Master of the Trim, he also has a knack for selecting investments. Of course, like the rest of us, he makes a bad trade from time to time, but has survived and flourished over the years, through a variety of market environments. One of his trades was quite a stand-out, and due to its stark simplicity, is particularly germane to our discussion.

One day in early 1979, a customer made the comment to him that "You ought to buy silver." A couple of months later, this same individual, back in for another haircut, once again said the same thing. Further inquiry established that the tipster was in the wholesale jewelry and dinnerware trade. Doug decided to take the plunge and scoured local coin shops, purchasing several thousand ounces of bullion rounds and "junk silver". The spot price at the time was around $18/ounce.

About 6 months later, said customer returned to the shop and as Doug was cropping his hair, commented, "You should **sell** your silver." Soon thereafter, Doug sold out his position at the prevailing price, which was close to $40 per ounce. Trade Closed.

Not complicated. Not Sexy. But very profitable. You probably know someone – perhaps several who, during the '70s, bought silver at $6, rode it up to $50, then back down to $5. They held on to their metal resolutely, missing every opportunity over the years to sell as prices stair – stepped in both directions.

Doug did not subscribe to a chart publication, nor pay for a market timing service. He didn't spend much time trying to "understand" the market. He just listened to what he heard. He paid attention to information which seemed to have the "ring of truth" - it felt right in the gut. When the time came that it felt right to sell, he simply followed the old Nike commercial's advice, "Just Do It."

Exit Strategy #7: "Gimme some 'o that Yahoooo!"

Here's another example illustrating a similar principle, which took place at the apex of the 2000 dotcom mania. A broker friend had among his clients, a wealthy farmer. You may know the type. They roll into town on Saturday in a beat up pickup, dressed in old work clothes to buy groceries. Most people assume they are just poor hayseeds. However, some of them are millionaires many times over!

The broker had been trying to get this particular customer to purchase some bonds being issued by the local school district – as safe a play as one could make. The farmer just wasn't interested. Then one day he called in to the broker and exclaimed breathlessly, "Gimme' some o' that Yahoooo!" -the Internet stock which, along with hundreds of other dotcoms was believed to be a tree destined for growth to the sky.

A month later, the NASDAQ, of which Yahoo was a component, topped and began a sickening slide that would eventually erase over two-thirds of its market value. Yahoo, at the time trading at $108 a share, tanked with the rest of the tech and financial sectors to well less than $5 (unlike many of its brethren however, it *is* still in business). We don't know when or if the farmer sold, but he did buy a chunk of stock, exactly 0.18 cents from the top!

The lesson is that when a person with whom you have spoken to for years about the merit of silver investing, and who never bought an ounce, finally decides to buy some and tells you why—take the cue - it's probably time to begin exiting your position.

Technical Analysis can help you say "Good-bye" - Successfully

A variety of technical analysis (TA) tools can help us get a handle on if we should be giving serious considering to exiting the market. Whether in tranches (portions), by offsetting certain holdings in their entirety, or going so far as to pare the overall portfolio to the bone in order to protect as much profit as possible. You could make the study and utilization of these tools a full time job, but we're not here to give you another job. If you need more detail on a specific tool, or perhaps want to try something we don't mention at all, Edwards and Magee should be your go-to learning source.

Please keep this idea in mind - The more TA signals that confirm an assumption, the greater confidence an investor can have in his/her decision-making about a trade. Also, keep an eye out for "non-confirmations". (e.g. a price keeps advancing, while MACD shows decreasing momentum, and declining Money Flow.). Non-confirms do not mean that immediate action is necessary, but at the very least, caution, along with further observation may be warranted.

Over the years, we've found the following TA indicators to be particularly helpful in a variety of market conditions, during both bear and bull markets. Just remember that their use helps, but does not replace other elements in the decision-making process. We'll need all the clues we can get in our efforts to make - and keep - substantial market profits.

Of Particular note:

Wedges - Ascending - (angle-dependent) are generally bearish/ descending, bullish.

Flags - A steep rise (or fall) creates a flag pole. As the flag "unfurls", prices should leave the pennant and continue in the direction of the original move within 2 wks.

Gaps - Especially informative in liquid markets, where high volume makes them a rarity - often, but not always filled. Common, breakaway, continuation, exhaustion and island.

Moving Averages - Especially 50 day, 200 day, 400 day and 20 month. The most carefully-observed lines are how the 50 Day and 200 Day MAs interact. A stock's price is considered to be in an uptrend when the 50 Day is above the 200 Day and both are rising.

Money Flow Indicator- measures how much money is going into a stock - charts back over months and years. Inflows (as well as controlled selling) are the lifeblood of a stock's rise. Some use this as an indicator of overbought and oversold conditions. Money Flow can serve as confirmation or non-confirmation in relation to other indicators.

MACD - price momentum measured and compared via a base-of-chart histogram.

Bollinger Bands-price envelopes within which a stock trades. When the bands compress, it indicates a probable breakout up or down, which may then be followed (It may take awhile for the breakout to get underway.). When prices exceed the outer boundaries of the envelope, they usually retreat back within its confines shortly thereafter, even if the direction of the intermediate move remains unchanged.

Two especially significant TA indicators to watch when expecting a long-term top:

Number One: The *Key Reversal* indicator in Technical chart analysis is defined as a day/week/month wherein the price of a stock or commodity trades higher <u>and</u> lower than the preceding day/week/month, and in the case of a potential new uptrend, closes above the preceding session's range. Some chartists also specify that (in the case of a presumed new uptrend) the Open must be above the previous session's close as well. Additional factors adding "confidence" to the analysis:

- A wide range day – the bigger the better (cleans out the opposing forces).
- The reversal takes place along with high trading volume
- A large amount of short covering, combined with new buying.
- MACD turning or running in the new direction.
- Similar action by other stocks in the sector
- A close above/strong move towards the 50/200 Day Moving Averages.
- Occasionally - especially early in a move - a Key Reversal provides a *false* signal.
- Key Reversal(s) holding on a longer basis – e.g. weekly/monthly/ yearly.

Additional confirmation takes place during successive days/weeks if the reversal day is not penetrated in the opposite direction on a closing basis. Ideally, "retracements" should not "eat up" more than one-half to two-thirds of the reversal session's price range (for our purposes, of the up move). *Key Reversals have more validity when they occur after a lengthy move.*

Number Two: The *Island Reversal* indicator occurs infrequently in TA, but when it does, you want to pay particular attention. An Island Reversal is a one or two day price range that trades beyond the price action on either side, leaving price gaps. In a top area, prices gap up, trade for one – three days, then gap back down. Except in thinly traded markets these formations are rare, but for the technician, it may offer a powerful clue about where the price may now be headed.

When you spot a possible island reversal, there are a couple of "good news" aspects about it. First, you'll know within a few days, whether or not it is valid. If the gaps get filled in either direction, then by definition the island has been invalidated. Second, you may have been given a limited-risk way to trade against, or "fade" market action.

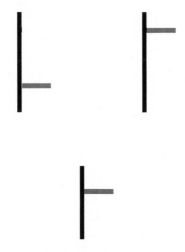

One-day Island Reversal (Steven A. Smith)

Let's say the price of silver On Day One closes on its low at $45. Day Two, the high-low-close is $44 - $38.75 - $43.50. On Day Three, silver gaps up on the open, trading at $45.25, keeps rising and closes at $46.00. Since no trading took place between $44.00 and $45.00, a (potential) one-day island reversal has been created.

You might choose to take or add to a position in support of the presumed reversal as it is being formed! On Day Three, you could place an order to buy no lower than the open, with your stop in the middle of Day Two's price range. If the gap is filled on the downside, you will be stopped out with a small loss. If it remains unfilled a for few days, a MAJOR low (or high) has probably occurred. Prices should then move aggressively away from the island formation, not returning for months or even years.

Imagine getting a fill at $46, and watching silver rise to $75, $100, $125 the ounce - a circumstance we believe is entirely possible going forward.

Island Reversal Indicators

- On a weekly/monthly chart, offers a strong signal of a long term top/bottom.
- Accuracy is added if accompanied by very high trading volume.
- Accuracy is further added if accompanied by an exhaustion gap.

Important TA use caveats

Many aspects of technical analysis - somewhat like looking at the "pictures" clouds form - have a tendency of being highly interpretative. Sometimes, several people can look at the same chart and see different things. All sub-disciplines in the field, be they studies of Candlesticks, Bar charts, Elliot Waves, Point and Figure, or other schools - sometimes identified by the name of the founder - involve correctly applying the science of the techniques, *as well as* the artistry of the person interpreting them. In addition, always remember that if the price acts the way "it's supposed to" by definition of the signal, then it can be considered attendant, or expected.

If it does not, the signal, also by definition has been invalidated. For example, the price you follow may have broken out of a triangle to the downside, reversed after a few days, and moved back into or even above the apex of the formation. Having done so, it could now have become prognostic, or predictive of an opposite situation.

2 Professional behaviors

Professionals pay more attention to horizontal lines of support and resistance lines (HSRs), than to angled trend lines, which are often falsely penetrated. Silver loves to do this.

Now comes one of the most important analytical rules of all, which only seems contradictory on the surface - that there really are no rules. If more traders had looked at things from this angle, they might have acted and stayed on the 2016 multi-month upside mining stock shock-wave, and ridden it straight into the first big correction (after at least 6 smaller previous ones) in late August of that same year.

We think it's worth your time to consider that there are really no absolutes in market analyses. It's a game of probabilities. Analysts of every stripe - including us - merely seek, via a myriad of approaches, to move that needle from the left, (chance) as far to the right (absolute accuracy) as possible.

When mining stocks make an important (intermediate - long term) top, <u>many</u> of them will print a similar-looking pattern.

There's little need to spend time thinking about "conspiracies" or "market manipulation." But we should recognize that all market participants have a view/preference about where prices are or should be headed, and by stepping onto the field, they become participants in those price movements. To a certain extent, Chris Powel of GATA speaks more than an element of truth when he says that "there are no markets, just manipulations." By definition, government entities with their geopolitical agendas at certain price and emotion points, are often the 800 pound gorillas of the market place.

The whole story is really of wider scope, because ultimately *The Market* is bigger than all the manipulators put together, whether they act singularly or in concert. Yes, their behavior can influence a trend, break certain rallies and declines, and even help force unexpected waterfall declines, like what we saw on several occasions during the extended gold and silver bear markets of 2011-late 2015. But on balance, the market inevitably reasserts itself, moving to its own beat in the direction its primordial energy dictates. And the longer and more powerful the distortion, the more violent will be the reaction in the opposite direction once the reset gets going.

It may take longer than we as investors/speculators would like, but Mr. Market always has the last word. In the interim, we just need to respect all of the forces moving back and forth on the marketplace battlefield, responding in such a way that we don't get killed before what we're pretty sure is going to happen actually takes place! Remember, the first part of the ancient but still relevant saying from Sun Tzu,

"If you know your opponent <u>and</u> yourself, you will be victorious in one hundred battles."

The preceding discussion has presented strategies for getting out (rather than being taken out) with a large portion of your profits, health and sanity intact during the closing phase of a bull market. It can provide reinforcement/clarification to what you may already know, as well as spark an interest in researching one or more concepts not previously considered.

Consider this to be a trading plan where involvement in precious metals investing becomes a *finite* as opposed to an infinite activity. Helping you to stay with the trend, as long as possible, take as much profit from it as can reasonably be expected - but not encouraging you to remain there indefinitely. And certainly not to ride it back down the way so many other investors are fated to do.

Like a fitness regimen, it will be up to the reader to mix/match/carry out a personal game plan in accordance with his/her unique perspective, personality and skills. It is presented in the spirit of inquiry and understanding, because it has also helped us to clarify our own reasons for market involvement. It bears repeating what Robert Bishop, past editor of the *Gold Mining Stock Report,* wrote when he reflected upon mining stock investing, commenting,

"Until the recent cycle, I never realized what I now regard as the simple truth of resource stock investing: there are times to be in the market, and times to be out of the market. Period."

We're often asked why would we (the precious metals') investor, ever cash out of our gold and silver, in exchange for paper? First, this chapter deals primarily with paper gold and silver claims; therefore you are trading one type of paper for another. Second, you can probably agree that there will come a time when alternate categories where you can deploy the cash quickly, pay off debt, buy something you really need/want, or find another unloved investment opportunity will become available - and appealing.

Preparing for the End of the Secular Gold and Silver Bull

During the eventual precious metals-mining stock blow-off phase, which may be several sub-phases, the level of irrationality will increase, as will price volatility. In the futures market for instance, a series of limit up and down days will become the norm. Even a trader with the presence of mind to employ coverage via a straddle or by shorting similar commodities on different exchanges could still be pulverized during this process. Thus you must be willing to accept the loss of the remaining position in its entirety, in exchange for a chance at grabbing a share of what may become the final convulsive gasp of a market one step removed from keeling over for good.

All traders, except those with the deepest pockets would be well-served to avoid margin like the plague. There can now be little doubt, that we are facing – for the first time in history – a global bull market in the precious metals. The swings on the way to the eventual top and thereafter, will almost certainly be of an epic scale.

Getting back in if a major top is forming, or later turns out to have been in place, is extremely dangerous. Prices tend to fall several times faster than they rise. In such a scenario, you can give back profits in a few weeks that may have taken months... or years to accumulate.

The Klondike Gold Rush Syndrome

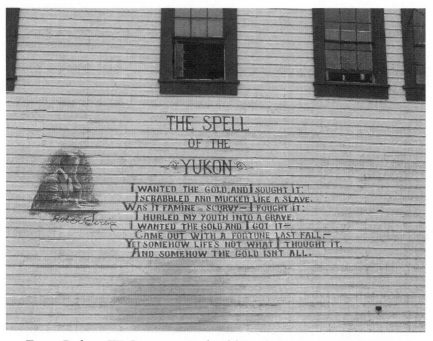

From Robert W. Service on a building in Dawson City, Yukon

The Last Great Gold Rush, 2000 - 20__?

Pierre Berton's seminal work on the Klondike Gold Rush has as part of its title, "The Last Great Gold Rush." Gold was discovered along the Klondike River in 1896. The following year, word of the remote strike reached the outside world, and newspaper reporting created a world-wide hysteria. Over the next two years, into 1899, as many as 100,000 would-be miners from around the world began the journey to the Klondike region of north-western Canada, in the area centered around present-day Dawson City, Yukon.

Because of the short travel season, harsh terrain, and requirements by Canadian authorities that to avoid starvation, each prospector had to bring along a ton of supplies, it took the majority who made it an additional year - into 1898 - to reach the gold fields. Once there, in a search for the illusive metal, they had to contend with the weather, permafrost, and each other. Men and women from all walks of life braved incredible hardship in order to pan for gold, or dig it out of the ground and run it through sluice boxes.

Less than a third of them made it to Dawson City. Of those who did, (according to research conducted by historynet.com) only about 4,000 struck "pay dirt". A select few became fabulously wealthy... for a time. Of those, most frittered away fortunes in saloons or speculations on roll-of-the-dice mining properties. It doesn't appear that many (any?) of them had a financial plan. What would come afterwards for them if they struck it big?

An interesting fact is that around half of those who succeeded in making it to the gold fields never even mined for gold! A lot of different factors must have been driving these "prospectors". *Why did they subject themselves to such a struggle? What was their motivation? Did they ever ask themselves, "How much would be enough for me?"*

We would argue that what the world experiences during the coming years will prove that Berton *almost* got it right. Whereas the 1898 gold mania can be seen as the penultimate, or second largest event of its kind, the coming gold-silver-miner shock-wave will be by far the greatest one of all!

Most of you really want to participate in the final phase of this gold and silver rush, but consider the risks. What's the real driver of your desire to become involved? Do you have a plan for getting out? What will you do with your earnings? When will you leave the game?

It's a bit about timing

If our timing is right, many of those reading this book will be operating in a continuum analogous to that of the prospectors headed for Klondike Gold Rush. Looking back, 2016 will be seen as the year the new bull leg began, with gold and silver rising 30% and many of the miners rocketing off bear market lows by several hundred percent. It will be the year that 21st century "prospectors" struck gold.

2017 becomes "the year of public recognition." Articles, and later books about how to "get wealthy in resources" will increasingly flood the marketplace, your mail box and inbox. Due to "the climate", "rugged terrain" and the spiraling cost and availability of physical precious metals, new investors will increasingly be drawn to buying mining stocks and ETFs in an effort to get onboard the bull run. By 2018, public participation will have become a major factor, leading to off-the-charts volatility in resource sector stocks. Will demand and higher prices keep the trend alive for several more years?

All of this will be happening for very authentic reasons. Physical metals' supply constraints. Unresolved problems from the 2008 global near-financial meltdown. Generational shifts as The Fourth Turning works its way through our lives. A search by Millennials to find a financial venue which might earn them a large payback from a modest investment over an intermediate time-frame. An effort by Baby Boomers to make up for a lost decade of earning almost no interest on money market and savings accounts.

Continued financial malfeasance on a global basis, as the activities of central banks and major financial houses drive us deeper into debt via paper/digital money creation and new layers of derivatives creation. Not to mention the imperative of rulers everywhere - retention and expansion of personal power and control. Things have become so distended, that as one of the great writers and social philosophers of our day, Robert Ringer puts it,

> "Only a fool believes that any government on earth
> is "of the people, by the people, and for the people."
> Government is — and has always been — of the

politicians, by the politicians, and for the politicians. That's why major changes occur only through violent revolution. Only the barrel of a gun can change the hearts and minds of men."

Let's hope that Ringer overstates the case. On the other hand, more often than not he's had history on his side...

Too late to get onboard? Not by a long shot. Don't forget that for the most part, these companies are still trading at a fraction of their 2011 highs - which in many cases are still 80% below those levels! With gold trading hundreds of dollars beneath its 2011, $1,923 high and silver well below its top print just below $50 - there would seem to be quite a bit of upside left!

A recovery by the miners and metals only takes us back to those intermediate peaks. What do you think will happen to the share prices of mining stocks and ETFs when gold and silver rocket to new nominal highs well above $2,000 and $50 respectively? It is our firm belief - phrasing it as a Canadian would - that this scenario is "written in the rocks".

By the time you've finished reading this book, gone through the thinking procedures we discuss and studied the tactics and tools to use, you'll know what to do and how to do it. By the time you've looked around you, and reflected deeply within yourself, you will have come to more fully understand your motivation. Than make a plan. Decide what you want to accomplish, how you're going to do it, and what your end game might look like. After that, all that remains is to Act!

While you're still in the process of thinking things through, keep in mind an old Chinese admonition - "Coming events cast their shadows before them."

Cashing out?

As far as cashing out of the real metal, it certainly can, and perhaps should be done when the value (purchasing power) is measured in real terms. Cashing out all of your holdings before the monetary system/ financial markets have been reset to a trustworthy mode may dictate holding some metal, but exchanging one real asset that is overvalued, for another real asset that is undervalued is how important wealth is ultimately built and preserved. Think of that "tide... in the affairs of man".

<u>We fully expect that when the time comes where we at *The Morgan Report* make our call to lighten up, the amount of negative comments coming our direction will set records. Nonetheless, with our having been through the last bull market and being obsessed with this one, you might want to consider re-reading this chapter when that day seems to be drawing near.</u>

It is our sincere belief that ignoring such an observation will ultimately and assuredly lead precious metals investors into the valley of fatigue, emotional despair and great financial loss. Consider leaving the party early with most of your winnings.

Exit Strategy # 10: "The Rule of the Book"

One of this writer's respected friends is a retired psychiatrist, a devotee of Albert Ellis. He likes to talk about the "Rule of the Book." The Book is your life; most of us get just one. The chapters of our "book" are the various activities and experiences we have along the way, as we "write" it. In the case of many people who never quite master the mainsprings of their existence, their book is largely written <u>for</u> them. The Rule of the Book is simple and is stated thus: When you have completed a chapter; write another!

It is possible to spend an entire life-time wrapped around an activity. It can be a matter of choice, born of free will, and who can fault us? But many people keep on with something, well past the point when the accrued benefits have paled in relation to the effort being expended. Sometimes we keep on because our identity has become mirrored by the activity. Sometimes the need to maintain it overwhelms our desire to do anything else. Most people never get around to asking themselves, "Why am I still doing this?" "Is this all there is?"

You probably know someone who spends 3 hours/day weight training at the gym. What may have started out as beneficial in pursuit of overall fitness and strength-training for betterment in life's other activities somehow becomes an end in itself. The original purpose has become obscured or forgotten.

Active investing is an energy-intensive and time-consuming, "life-time" wasting activity. If done for some reason other than to accumulate lucre, shouldn't there be a plan for an "end-game?" Is it unreasonable to think about when one might step aside and do something else with the finite years one has left on this plane?

A small-town retailer takes his vocation for giving value, variety and service to the customer, turns it into the largest volume chain of department stores in the world, and keeps growing the business, even as he is felled by cancer. Another begins with a small television station and parlays his stake into a fortune worth $8 billion; then watches it shrink to less than $1billion.

Two brothers move into silver and "hard investments." When the bubble breaks, they proceed to lose what may have been the largest family fortune in American history.

Trees don't grow to the sky. Balance sheets don't keep increasing forever. Lives are finite. Given this, maybe there is a time when each of us should start to write another chapter.

The next chapter defines and discusses how to build and use the Sacrifice Throw Portfolio (STP) as the ultimate investment act in the current Precious Metals' secular bull market. Its premise is that you should be able to capture a large chunk of the total run – just like the "sandwich trader" does, AND remain positioned with a defined amount of risk capital, so that you stay connected with what may still be an ongoing bullish trend!

CHAPTER 10

Leave the Wave, Part II:
The "Sacrifice Throw" Portfolio

"The upshot is that juniors with proven, accessible deposits don't really have to do much from here on out. They can just hang around and wait for the offers to roll in. Before it's over, they'll be the dotcoms of this generation." **-John Rubino**

"Five Minutes"

During WWII, known by Japan as "The Fifteen Years War", the inflection point - the point of no return - came in 1942 at the Battle of Midway. Two fleets across the horizon from each other prepared to do battle. The Japanese aerial strike force had just returned from bombing the US base at Midway and was rearming on deck for another sortie, when their fleet carriers were attacked by an American sea-launched torpedo bombing squadron. Japan's Combat Air Patrol shot down every last American plane, with no damage to the fleet. Only now they realized that, rather than just land-based planes from Midway, there was also an enemy fleet with which to contend.

Rearm with torpedoes instead of land bombs? The decision was made. So on that fateful day, four of Japan's largest carriers, with hundreds of its best pilots, worked feverishly, removing bombs and installing torpedoes, in preparation for an attack on the American fleet whose coordinates and distance were still unknown to them.

Then it happened. Out of the sky, almost by accident another American bombing force had spotted the fleet. Japanese CAP was still just above the waves and could do nothing to stop the onslaught. The decks were covered with ordnance, aviation fuel and personnel. Within 5 minutes, all 4 carriers were ablaze from end to end, and by nightfall, each would come to rest on the ocean's bottom. For three more years the bloody fighting continued, but because of Midway's "tipping point", the strategic initiative and the back of Japan's carrier forces had been broken.

Historical inflection points abound. With the 300 Spartans at Thermopylae, and the Greek sailors in the sea battle of Salamis, where Athenian Triremes shattered the fleet and with it, dreams of the Persians, ensuring the evolution of European culture. For the Romans and the Carthaginians at the battle of *Cannae* enabling another 1000 years of Roman history. On the Golan Heights, when 5 IDF tanks outnumbered 20 to 1 broke the assault of Syrian armour, granting control of this vital area to Israel up through the present day.

"There is a moment in a battle when the least movement brings decisive victory. A single drop makes the cup runneth over."- Napoleon Bonaparte

At some point during the next number of years, when the cycle of what may come to be known as the greatest precious metals bull market of all time prepares to turn, a magic moment will take place. Time will stand still --when "a single drop makes the cup runneth over." The gold and silver bull will have been mortally wounded though the participants won't know it – yet. It will have come at a place where price intersects with an event - or a series of them, fueled by the psychology of the marketplace.

After that time, even as thousands of pitched battles between buyers and sellers rage, everything will have been unalterably and permanently changed. How can we as investors "panic first and beat the rush" to the bolt hole?

Some of you have subscribed to *The Morgan Report,* listened to David Morgan speak at conferences, or possibly followed him on YouTube since the precious metals' bull market got underway in 2000. If so, you know that one of his most important and frequently-stated mantras (after "buy physical first") is that 80-90% of the profit potential of the entire secular run is likely to take place during the last 10% (in time) of the move. It's when the public mania – and paranoia- will be running at full force, when prices that took years to double, now triple or quadruple in months, weeks…or days! All the top-callers are being discredited and humbled as the market blasts higher.

Major financial magazines and newspapers carry lead stories about the wisdom of buying gold and silver; they discuss how the financial system is inevitably nearing collapse; how "a new bi-metallic monetary standard" is being discussed in Congress; how major banks are in default because the leased-gold contracts they hold, have 100 claims against them for every ounce of actual gold and silver they have in stock - and you'll be told that the proof of this is finally coming to light due to whistle-blowers at banks or major brokerage houses.

Before the fall…

During the last innings - perhaps even into "overtime", big price drops will continue to be seen as "buying opportunities." Price gaps - areas on the charts where no trading takes place - will become common even in highly liquid share issues, in ETPs, in the physical metals' spot and futures contracts themselves. First common gaps show up, then breakaway gaps, followed by continuation gaps. Late in the primary move, exhaustion gaps - points where new buying is barely sufficient to power prices higher – start appearing. More and more people are now "marching in the parade" even as fewer are on the sidelines watching the procession. Finally, at the end, either the key reversal - or the island reversal - the deadliest (and one of the most reliable, once confirmed) of all gaps to be found in technical analysis is likely to step onstage.

This is very important. When a new bull run has gotten underway - be it the initial few years' thrust into 2006, the major up move out of the 2008-09 global near-debacle, or the 2016 powerful rise from January - August, 2016 that fooled almost all the experts, there's a fairly consistent pattern the mining stock sector goes through. First the junior producers start powering upward, then the majors, and third, the smaller issues and exploration stocks. During that initial move out of the gates, you'll see scattered strength in most/all the legitimate operations, but eventually they'll be rising in the order just described.

Finally as the up-move matures, "pigs will fly". Internet promoters will heavily saturate your Inbox and snail mail boxes with a "once-in-a-lifetime opportunity" offered by an exploration or marginal producer company you've probably never heard of before. Those "pump and dump" plays, bought into mostly by the uninformed, will finally show chart strength and double or triple in price before their inevitable collapse.

What The Ultimate Top will look like.

When the first intermediate term shakeout occurs, the companies trading with thin volume will gyrate wildly in both directions, placing money into the pockets of shills, as their share price bid-ask spread widens appreciably. This latter action takes place even before the "Big Top" event we'll all be watching for that marks the penultimate, if not the ultimate top of the decades' long precious metals'/miners' bull run.

When the last rally (rallies) fizzle out, the entire sector could go into a steep, lasting downtrend. However, if gold is used to mitigate the financial crisis as the precious metals soar, this would most likely stabilize the producing miners at some level. If this does not happen during or shortly after the next "crisis", the most likely path is what happened last time, in all other overvalued markets.. at which time - ALL miners will start to fall together. The few which levitate briefly will be the exception to the rule... and soon thereafter they too will begin their decline. The better issues will fall a bit slower, rally more frequently, and overall, hold up better. But keep in mind that almost every issue will be moving into the pattern of intermediate to long term downtrends, as market sentiment turns from hyper-optimism to concern, to fear - and once again these stocks become undervalued.

(If you have any doubts about what happens in a severe downturn, go back to the charts for just about any company you're following and look at what happened to them during the 2011-15 downturn. We rest our case.)

After the top, dozens, scores, even hundreds of mining sector companies will show almost identical chart topping patterns. Island tops; key reversals; ascending (bearish) wedges; downside breakouts from flat -based triangles.

By then, just about every precious metals analyst will have built a case that that "this time it's different" because gold and silver have reached a new level, the prices below which "we'll never see again in our lifetimes". "We're running out." These analysts <u>will</u> be right…but for the wrong reason.

<u>What's **really** running out is the time you have to turn "paper profits" - what you've earned that's still at risk in the market - into real profit.</u> Dollars and cents lodged in the cash account of your brokerage statement that you could buy something with, gift to someone, or even withdraw and bury in the back yard!

At the beginning of this book, we took the position that during the coming few years, we would witness a bull market run to a peak in the metals that would truly be "one for the record books".

Risk? You bet. Reward? Yes, a lot of that too. As a Canadian talk show host commented a few years ago, "All things worth doing have two elements – Fear and excitement." If you think you can handle *both* of these elements, then step up to the plate!

This Time it *is* Different!

This time it really will be different. The potential number of market participants will be ten times greater than during the 1980's bull market. Eventually, as the aged bull rolls over and heads for the depths, a lucky and prepared few will safely step aside, like one passenger did when the stern of the doomed Titanic slipped silently beneath the waves.

These relative few will be able to do so because they will hold a much different mindset than the rest. Their outlook will help separate them from the effects of the "extraordinary popular delusions and the madness of crowds" about which Charles Mackay referred in his seminal work of the same name. Like the endlessly-honed skills of Japan's most famed samurai, Miyamoto Musashi, whose katana blade divined its point of impact even before being drawn from the *saya* (scabbard), the prepared, assured and balanced investor will "think only of the cut". <u>We want you to be among those who end up in that mega-successful group!</u>

Think only of the Cut...

Do You Know Yourself?

The great Chinese military strategist Sun Tzu wrote:

If you know your opponent and yourself, you will be victorious in one hundred battles.
Know only yourself, and the odds are even.
If you know neither, there is great danger in one hundred battles.

This time it's going to be profoundly different for the investor who builds and successfully implements the uniquely, personalized, previously-decided-upon components of his/her Sacrifice Throw Portfolio (STP). Investors will have a reasonably good understanding of their "opponent" – a riotous collection of participants motivated by successive waves of fear and greed. By planning ahead, and having formed a habit of working through the OODA Loop, these investors will have an almost unbelievably better understanding of themselves and their relationship to the coming market vortex than all but the smallest minority of those who will populate the marketplace battlefield.

The "Sacrifice Throw" as an Exit Strategy

In a Judo match, opponents grasp each other's lapel with one hand, with the other hand holding the competitor's sleeve. As the pair moves across the tatami mats, the goal is to effect *kuzushi* - the breaking of the opponent's balance, leading to an attempted foot sweep or throw. A clean throw is awarded an *ippon!* ending the match.

There is a throwing technique called *tomoe-nage*, which in Japanese means "round throw", "stomach throw", or "sacrifice throw". It's called this because the thrower (*Tori*), after weakening his opponent's balance (*kuzushi*), drops down onto his back, pulling his opponent down toward him as he attempts, by placing one foot into his adversaries' midsection, to launch him (*Uke*) over/behind himself onto the mat.

The Sacrifice Throw-Tomoe Nage (Courtesy Steven A. Smith)

He "sacrifices" his stance, his upright position, and his ability to attempt other types of sweeps or throws in order to hopefully catapult his opponent through the air and score a decisive point (*Ippon*) for an instant win. A sharp competitor may counter by quickly stepping aside, or simply dropping down onto the thrower in order to effect a pin or choke – variations of which can also serve to defeat this sacrifice-to-win tactic.

Given the risk, a competitor who attempts this win-or-lose maneuver needs to fully understand the implications involved and do everything possible to "get it right" the first time. (A secondary consideration is that the throw might be partially effective, in which case *Tori* may be awarded a half-point or *waza ari*. Therefore, "winning" results can still be achieved by being even partially successful using this effective but risky technique.)

Looking back at 1980

Why should you consider constructing and using a Sacrifice Throw Portfolio (STP)?

Because no one – no matter how accomplished, can know when the ultimate market top is in until well after the fact. In January 1980, when gold peaked at around $850, very few participants believed they were witnessing gold's swan song. 20 years later, it traded below $300 the ounce, and it was not until 2008 – a full 28 years afterward, that gold would once again touch the nominal $850 level. What is even more discouraging is that, depending upon what measurement index is used, the inflation-adjusted price today would need to be at least 5 times as much…as in $3,000 - $5,000 – in order to equal its prevailing purchasing power at $850.

The potential to make – and keep – outsized gains during that final pricing window was open for the briefest of moments. Would you rather do everything possible to capture the lion's share of profit the market makes available to you into the last inning, and then Quit? Or act like most other investors, riding the elevator all the way up, and all the way down... for a generation?

Today there are powerful factors that can work in favor of the disciplined investor seeking to wring out as much profit as possible during the last act of this drama. A range of trading vehicles which did not even exist then, are now accessible by virtually anyone with a brokerage account containing a few thousand dollars. IF the category of surgical "double-edged swords" appeals to you - and they fascinate us (with equal amounts of intrigue and terror!) -then <u>be sure to re-read the ETF section</u> in order to have a well-grounded understanding before deciding to employ them.

The rationale for constructing and using a **Sacrifice Throw Portfolio (STP)** rests upon the following assumptions and considerations:

That:

- There is a time to say "Good Bye Mr. Market"
- The final bull market top is impossible to predict via price or time.
- The end of the secular bull-run will usher in a lengthy secular bear market.
- Thereafter, profitable cyclical swing trading will be difficult and time-consuming.
- Investors may consider deploying their winnings into other investment sectors.
- <u>The STP is to be considered 100% expendable.</u>

How it should work:

- Over time, sell core portfolio holdings (your primary and secondary stage rocket launch) in tranches, into vertical price movement.
- Allow your *Sacrifice Throw Portfolio* aka *Space Module* to continue upward - flying into "deep price space" in an effort to catch some of "the last one-eighth".
- Consider buying small amounts of short (inverse) metals ETFs into great strength.
- ** A variation of the above theme would be to wait for a 50% retracement back up toward the point of the initial break; then either offset the remaining Sacrifice Portfolio positions, or purchase leveraged inverse gold, silver and or mining stock ETFs.
- If your timing is incorrect, and the market collapses after making what appears to be the "Big Top" - if you're still "all in" with your STP, be prepared for the possibility of having to "sacrifice" it for a 100% loss. Leading up to this point, your subjective analysis of how much risk you're willing to take in order to achieve additional returns will need to be addressed.

Or:

- Let the STP ride until YOU decide to get out, selling into great strength – then offset completely - FOR GOOD. "Burn your charts" and have a "market-free" life.

Advantages: Historically, a person who believed the market was topping or had topped, and who wanted to try and make money on the downside, may have sold completely out and gone short. If they were too early, the portfolio draw down would be enormous. The great risk would be of losing much of what had been made in the primary portfolio during the entire bull market.

Some deep-pocket investors can handle the emotional/financial price for doing this. (Sir John Templeton, as mentioned, was one of the very few.) But for the rest of us, it's simply too much to deal with. Furthermore, once committed, there is no practical way of "remaining long" the market – you've given up the possibility of collecting ANY profit from further upside price movement.

Constructing the Sacrifice Throw Portfolio (STP):

<u>What follows is one way that an STP might look</u>. The elements chosen are less important than the concepts of how to build, maintain and utilize it. For example, you may not want to include a 3x leveraged ETF like **USLV**, preferring to use one, such as **SLV,** which more closely reflects the price movement of silver on a 1:1 basis (= lower volatility/risk). You might not feel comfortable with <u>ever</u> using an inverse ETF like the silver-leveraged UltraShort silver **ZSL,** the inverse-trading leveraged mining stock, **DUST**, or its Inverse 3x exploration stock index, **JDST.**

Further, you might decide to really "keep it simple" and include <u>only</u> individual mining stocks as your STP components.

The STP is envisioned to become activated during the timeframe in which the final stage of the precious metals' blow off/public mania phase is underway. By its nature this will involve <u>subjective</u> decision-making regarding component choices, weighting and offset timing.

The STP trader who employs this strategy is willing to "sacrifice" preselected holdings in exchange for the possibility of "getting a clean throw" (or two) of profits at considerably higher prices. The STP protocol envisions that by this time, the majority of the investor's profits **and** the initial stake from his/her core holdings will have been removed. <u>At a certain point, the STP will represent the entire precious metals'/resource sector holdings (excluding physical metal?) for that investor.</u>

Approaching it this way, an important psychological element has been removed from the individual's trading environment. With core positions completely offset, fear of loss will have been greatly minimized. While everyone else is caught up in the mass hysteria going on all around, you remain calm, cool and collected.

And finally, it bears repeating that those who build/use the STP, must resign themselves to the fact that, in seeking to capture "the last one-eighth" – or some portion of it – they are exposing their STP holdings to a total loss.

Special Notes:

- Whereas leveraged ETPs are fully acceptable for use as components in the STP, for the vast majority of investors, the use of margin should **not** be considered.
- Futures and options could be housed within the boundaries of an STP, but due to the vagaries of using them – e.g. backwardation, etc. when futures contracts are rolled over, extreme leverage/extreme volatility <u>their use is not covered in this discussion</u>.

"Loading" the STP

What follows is an <u>example</u> of how a "Model STP Portfolio" might look. Percentages are for illustration only - <u>The decisions on which elements and position percentages to include must be yours and yours alone.</u>

- Junior gold and silver producers: 30% <u>of STP account</u>
- Royalty Companies: 10 -15%.
- ETF Miners (e.g. SIL) (1:1 and/or 2 - 3:1 leveraged) 20%
- ETF Miners (1:1 and/or 2-3:1 leveraged/Inverse) 10%
- Exploration Companies: ("Pigs will fly")   10 -15%
- Cash: (Cash - a "trading vehicle" element)   10 - 0%

The following ETF "starter list" is a jumping off point for an investor to begin performing due diligence, before "loading" their own uniquely-designed and weighted STP. We suggest as part of your "discovery" process, that you check each entry to confirm adequate levels of daily volume. In our experience, absent highly volatile market conditions, Exchange Traded Products/Funds (ETPs) should have a bid-ask (b-a) spread of less than 5 basis points. Usually, it should only be 1-3bp b-a spread.

Sub-categories:

1:1 tracking Mining Share ETPs: GDX, GDXJ, SIL,
1:1 tracking Metals' ETPs: SLV, GLD, PALL, SIVR, PSLV
1:1 tracking Mining Shares ETPs: GDX, GDXJ, SGDM

2-3x tracking leveraged Metals' ETPs: AGQ, USLV,

Inverse 2-3x tracking Mining Shares ETPs: DUST, JDST, JNUG
Inverse 2-3x leveraged Metals' ETPs: ZSL, GLL (thin volume)

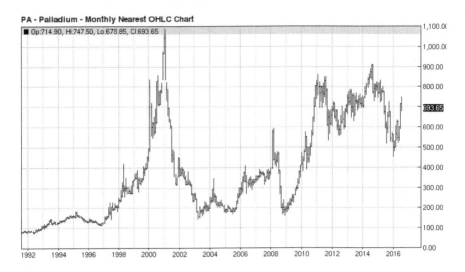

Monthly Palladium (Barchart.com)

Given silver's "restless nature", it could be a vertical affair similar to 1980, here looking at the palladium top which took place in 2001. The 25 year monthly chart shows what would almost qualify as a massive monthly island reversal – in this case, three months with no trading on either side.

It is worth noting in this chart that the majority of the culminating move came in a very short time frame! Again, this illustrates the idea of ninety percent of the move coming in the last ten percent of the time. However, getting out at the exact top of a parabolic move is almost impossible and what appears to look like selling too soon, may be determined upon reflection after the top has been achieved, to have been an excellent sell point.

An old floor trading homely states that "The market doesn't ring a bell at the top." Well, in the case of palladium's amazing 3 _month_ island reversal, we'd have to wonder… how could _anyone_ look at this chart and not suffer tinnitus from hearing bells tolling for this aged bull?

In platinum, when prices broke down through $800 (leaving an exhaustion gap on the upside and a breakaway gap into the decline) on the downside, it was all over for the next 16 years and counting.

"Beam me <u>out</u> Scottie" – What to Look For.

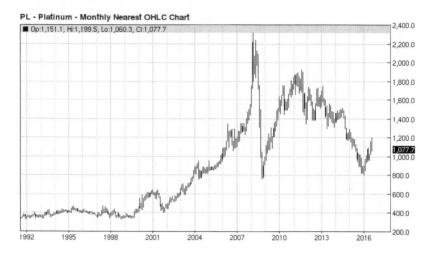

PL - Platinum - Monthly Nearest OHLC Chart

Op:1,151.1, Hi:1,199.5, Lo:1,060.3, Cl:1,077.7

Monthly Platinum (Courtesy Barchart.com)

Observing what happened to platinum, this chart referenced the 2008 all time high, fully$500/ounce above the 5 year chart previously shown. A trader would have had at least 6 months to have ridden/offset their STP between $1800 and $2200+. Consider the possibility that when silver achieves <u>its</u> all time high, it MAY print a chart pattern like this one. After dropping about 65%, it could then retrace 50% of its entire bull move – before heading lower for a generation.

It's possible, but <u>much less likely</u> that the last phase of this precious metals' bull market will end with a rounding top that takes awhile to form. This would give market participants quite a bit of time to sell into a series of rallies, as they challenged what would be looked back upon in retrospect at the bull market peak. This "best case scenario" is demonstrated in the 5 year platinum chart above. After the lofty top above $2200 and the ensuing waterfall decline into $800, Platinum built itself a bull market "echo" over the next two years. Then, over several months, a series of higher highs were registered until the ultimate reaction peak took place just above $1900. Frankly, we don't recall seeing another market which gave the buy and hold crowd this kind of "second chance" after such a collapse - and within such a relatively short time-frame

An investor selling out an STP into the highs just above $1,850 during the 2009-12 platinum bull run had three SETS of opportunities – each comprising several weeks, to have said "Good bye Mr. Market". Looking back from the second half of that same year, would getting completely out $20-$30 from the ultimate top have been "acceptable"?

Reading the Tea Leaves

When reading the tea leaves in an effort to get a handle on where the ultimate silver and gold tops may lie, we will be searching for two things: First, not necessarily where the ultimate top may or may not be forming. Rather we could find ourselves in circumstances where volatility has become so violent, that you to conclude staying with your Core positions has, from a risk-reward perspective, simply become too dangerous. "How could this be?"

In addition to the usual trading session during the day, the metals also have extended day, and then night sessions. Indeed, somewhere in the world they trade almost around the clock. As an example, something significant could take place at the Shanghai Gold Exchange (SGE). During the night session in North America, gold could experience a huge drop. Silver could plunge twenty percent. And that drop could sustain itself into the next morning's trading on the U.S. and Canadian exchanges. If the shock was severe enough, the speculation leading up to it inflated enough, the reasons (almost certainly) obscure enough, your mining stock, ETF, leveraged ETF portfolio could open down 30% on the day!

We could see in the resource sector, a session like what took place in 1987, when the U.S. stock market indices plunged 22%... in one day! Sure, maybe a year later, your losses might have been erased into a higher market like what happened by 1998. But don't count on it.

Just as when we employ technical analysis, we're looking for several clues that, taken as a group, may be telling us it's time to leave the party... altogether. Do not consider the following to be an all-inclusive list, nor have they been intentionally prioritized, but rather view them more like a "Chinese menu" where investors choose a number of items from the table, and upon placing them on their plate, have selected a "full-meal (analysis) deal."

No single, or even several elements below necessarily means that the metals' bull run is over. But they should be considered as warnings that the internal structure of the market is becoming more problematic. That it is becoming more susceptible to the countervailing force of an outside shock, which if hit with a secondary impact, could be enough to knock the bull to its knees - before delivering the coup de grâce.

- **The Dow/Gold Ratio:** the last two secular lows came in around 2:1 and 1:1 respectively (1 or 2 ounces of gold buying the Dow.) The forthcoming ratio could end up anywhere from 2:1 to perhaps 1/4:1 (One quarter ounce of gold buying a share each stock in the DJIA.) In the Internet age, the question becomes, how long would it hold?

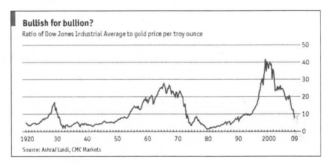

Ratio of DJIA vs. Gold (Ashraf Laidi CMC Markets)

- **Real Interest Rates (>2%):** This is a bit more obscure, because it is more of a lag indicator. In other words, it's difficult to know when the effect of this "rule" will affect metals in a meaningful way. Also one has to decide whether to use today's highly modified view of the CPI, which looks at inflation *vis à vis* interest rates, or to choose one of the earlier versions going back to 1980 as computed by John Williams at shadowstats.com. However, since most analysts, reporters and investors will be looking at the current CPI configuration, it might make sense to join them.

Google "trends/explore" looking at "gold investing" under "Interest over Time". Levels near 100 indicate a significantly overbought situation, whereas 25 or less may indicate an oversold/possible long addition. "Interest in silver - past 30 days" March, 2013 = 100; >60 = overbought? https://www.google.co.uk/trends/explore

- **A series of large SLV withdrawals**: plot these holdings over time for high/low balance reference? And/or concomitant with large GLD withdrawals.
- **The Silver/Gold Ratio:** The modern history tops so far of c. 97:1 were lodged in May, 1941 and February 1991. Modern low was <18:1 lodged in February, 1980. Pay particular attention, if/when the S/G ratio gets into the area of 25:1 or less.

The Dow/Silver Ratio: As far as we know, Steve St. Angelo "owns" this topic. You can find charts and a discussion on his site at https://srsroccoreport.com

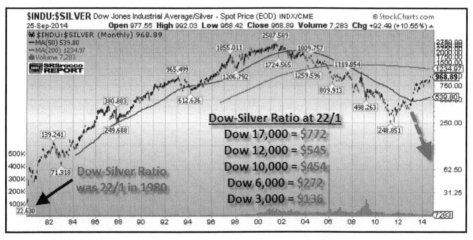

Dow-Silver Ratio 1980 - Present (Courtesy Steve. St. Angelo)

- **The $XAU:$Gold ratio** - Gold stock appreciation versus gold peaked in 1996 (after making a slightly lower peak in 1994). The first intermediate-longer term fan line to reverse this trend was created in early 2016. Once the ratio moves up convincingly we should have confirmation that the mega-downtrend, where gold outperformed mining shares has reversed. If/as this happens it will likely have major positive benefits to our strategy of seeking 10x + on mining stocks.

- **The Gold/Housing Ratio:** *The Gold/Housing ratio is a measure of relative value between gold and real estate. It is the number of ounces of gold required to purchase an average single family home in the United States. During the almost 5 decades that Americans have been allowed to own gold, it has taken an average of about 285 ounces of gold to purchase an "average" single family home.*(We don't know if this takes into consideration that the square footage of an "average" home may have increased over the years.)

- **Gold declining in other currencies vis á vis the USD.** (For almost two years before the 2015 lows were printed, the price of gold was rising in many other currencies. Will its decline on the way down foretell a long-term top?

- **The downside penetration of major horizontal support (HSR) line(s).** Most traders watch slanted trend lines, but if you look at what happened in 2012 after silver broke down below the HSR line around $26, you will see this was a major signal failure to hold support, with dire implications on the downside for the next few years. (Become very concerned about a 4th support challenge!) In addition, silver did so on the fourth attempt at penetration. Three attempts is one thing. But if a fourth try is in the works, it's not so good for the bulls.

- **A Narrow extended Bollinger Band, which may lead to a downside penetration** - especially after a lengthy period of "narrow bandwidth". The rule is to follow the direction of the breakout.

- **A 50% or larger Fibonnaci Retracement.** (Google for a full explanation.)

- **A wave of extended/massive public selling of physical silver**: We will likely see <u>several</u> of these selling waves on the way to silver's ultimate top. Until the end, they will merely temporarily bunt, rather than stop silver's meteoric ascent.

- **Large, consistent metal inflows to an exchange:** We are now in a global bull market – so the first sign of this <u>might be</u> on the Shanghai Gold Exchange (SGE), rather than the COMEX.

- **One (or a series) of Island Reversals** on the charts. The longer the measuring period, the greater the importance that should be assigned to such an occurrence. Therefore, whereas a daily island should get your attention (can also be a two-three day reversal), a weekly should cause your brows to furrow, and a monthly or yearly should make your hair stand on end!

- **The 400 Day** (and the exponential) **Moving Average** - For a continued bullish bias, you want to see metals' prices trading above this average.

- **Mining Chart Mirror Images ("schooling price behavior"):** At intermediate to major tops (and bottoms) in the mining sector, there is a tendency for company chart patterns to have a very similar look. Many companies will begin a decline almost simultaneously. It might be from a spike high-low close day, after several narrow range days of sideways trading, or occasionally, topping action may get underway by leaving a small gap to the downside. When you notice a particular pattern forming in some of your holdings, look at others in the same sector.

  Watch carefully for this on the charts. Such mining stock "schooling" price behavior should be duly noted. An intermediate (1-3 months) top may be in process, or it could signal the end of the entire secular run.

- *Silver trades below its 20 month Moving Average* - this indicator is written about by Analyst, Roland Watson, (Roland stated in correspondence with us that "The 20 month moving average is more useful as a buy signal, mainly due to the fact that silver spikes so sharply on a bull peak that most of the price is gone on a 20 month MA." Watson addresses the dilemma we all will face about deciding when to leave the market - and the implications if we don't get it reasonably correct, writing:

  "In my opinion, the next major peak will be the last for a generation as we finally enter that deflationary depression much heralded by the doom merchants. What the price of silver will be on that auspicious day is anyone's guess... My approach is simpler, when this indicator rings its bell; you get out without trying to form an opinion on whether the price is "too low" or the clarion calls of those who urge everyone to hold on for even greater profits. I just hope I am strong enough to follow through on that amidst the clamour! .... Silver is on the verge of big things in the years ahead. Don't waste (this monumental opportunity) by having no exit strategy!"

....

Conclusion: No matter how many of these indicators "line up", we need to remember that it is Mr. Market who <u>always</u> gets the last word. Bells ringing, fat ladies singing - something that hopefully gets our attention before the market turns down for the count.

The "hidden advantage" a miners/ETP portfolio segment gives you over physical silver sales, at/near "the top."

In 1980, long-side futures traders may have nailed down a price near the $50 silver top, but the average person's on the street sell-back may have only yielded $35-$40. This was in part because a LOT of physical silver was coming back from the public - jamming up the silver refining/sales pipeline. This time it "may be different" because the mania will be a global phenomenon, and numerous countries will be providing 2-way markets (i.e. buy-sell), it's possible that traders providing arbitrage will help lower the bid-ask spread to a more realistic - read fair to the customer who is selling - asking price when they want to turn in some of their silver. Would it not be discouraging to see, say $250 silver, yet only get $190 for some of yours? Let's hope this will not be the case.

(Re)Buyer Beware! - Avoid re-establishing a post-exit core position. This Bull Market will end <u>after</u> EVERY Top-Caller has been discredited!

There's something almost as bad as getting out of a sector or position too late. And maybe worse than getting out "a little too soon". It's about getting out way too early. In late 1998 and into 1999, several prominent analysts were advising getting out of the stock market because it had become "overvalued." Imagine if you had closed out your positions **a year** before the .com mania peaked in 2000. (Those last 4 years, the Dow was rising at 24%/annum. And then if you had been unable to stand watching the markets continue to go up for the next 18 months. So in early 2000, you threw caution to the wind and jumped back in...

This is not a good plan. And it's why we came up with the idea of the Sacrifice Throw Portfolio plan (STP). It will keep you in the game as long as you can stand the heat after you've safely "recused" the majority of your campaign's portfolio profits. It will offer you the chance of making - and hopefully keeping - additional profits with the remaining "space module" positions still at risk in the market.

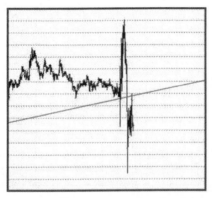

Volatility: The "gold sewing machine"
(Courtesy, Stu Thomson - Graceland Updates)

Once you've decided to (largely) exit the market...

You MUST - and this is absolutely critical... avoid re-establishing a post-exit <u>core</u> position. If you've followed our suggestions, you've already come to terms with the possibility of losing your entire STP, if you've overstayed your welcome into "the top". This understanding should enable you to be considerably more relaxed about working the STP, or simply letting things run, until you the time comes when you can no longer answer in the affirmative, the question, "Do I feel lucky today?" That's when you either start offsetting tranches of positions into great strength, or simply blow the remaining holdings out "at the market."

When you're tempted to go back in, answer this question... How Much (for You) is Enough? And ask yourself again about what drove you to invest in the resource sector in the first place. Then be sure to answer the question - "How much of what I have earned, do I want to give back to Mr. Market?"

Dénouement

One last fundamental consideration-- try not to let the desire for investment success overwhelm the need of attending to the really meaningful pursuits and relationships in your life. Indeed, the idea of devoting just the amount of time necessary on this market play should resonate with the reality that we have a finite amount of time to spend on this plane.

Being willing to say "Good bye Mr. Market" well before you have to bid adieu – perhaps involuntarily to your eviscerated trading funds - and to the other activities in your life, makes sense well above the potential extra amount of dollars and cents you might have been able to pick up from the trading floor by overstaying your welcome.

Felix Dennis, one of the UK's wealthiest men, wrote in his autobiography:

> "I have been very poor, and am now very rich. I am an optimist by nature. And I have the ability to write poetry and create the forest I am busy planting. Am I happy? No. Or, at least, only occasionally, when I am walking in the woods alone, or deeply ensconced in composing a difficult piece of verse, or sitting quietly with old friends over a bottle of wine. Feeding a stray cat...I could do all those things without wealth."

Asian cultures have historically understood and appreciated the impermanence of all things. Westerners may see this as a pessimistic outlook, but it does confer upon us a certain freedom of action - offering us the option of living - and appreciating all things - in the moment. Offering us the chance to be thankful for what's in our hands, in our vision, in our hearts at that second. The opportunity to express gratitude for the temporal provisions we're given. We wish all of our readers the clarity of being grateful for the profits they achieve and the lessons they have learned.

"The sounds of the (Gionshoya) bell echoes the temporary nature of all things. The color of the flowers of the teak tree declares that they who flourish must be brought low. The ones are but for a moment, like an evening dream in springtime. The mighty are destroyed; at last they are but as the dust before the wind."

(Helen Craig McCullough -The Tale of the Heike)

Whether you exceed your financial goals by a factor of 20, or end up with less than where you began, at life's end you - like the rest of us - will be left with but one thing — Memories. May your decisions beforehand and your reflection upon them afterwards bring you both satisfaction and quietude.

Final Thoughts: Some readers may question selling metal for fiat "dollars." This consideration can certainly be justified because so much is at stake in the current financial system. The idea of the U.S. dollar going to absolute zero is possible but unlikely. The Morgan Report team will provide website members with our current thinking when a sell decision is finally made. The main point for you is to decide ahead of time what you wish to do with your profits. Some will want to invest into another sector, others may wish to start a business, purchase real estate, or simply lead a quiet life. Since there will be such emotion surrounding the demise of the current monetary system, we suggest that you continue your education and plan ahead.

major conventions put on by Cambridge House, Sprott Asset Management, Resource Consultants, Stansberry and Associates, and others. And always remember, that no matter where you get the information necessary to move you towards a go/no go investment decision, "Do the Research. Do the Math. The Decision Must be Yours!"

CHAPTER 12

The Final Turn: Where Precious Metals, Millennials, and Boomers Intersect

*"There is no fire like passion, there is no shark like hatred, there is no snare like folly, there is no torrent like greed." – **Gautama Buddha***

In 1997, Neil Howe, historian, economist and demographer, along with William Strauss, published *The Fourth Turning: An American Prophecy - What the Cycles of History Tell Us About America's Next Rendezvous with Destiny*. It is our belief that *The Fourth Turning* offers an intriguing view of where we as a nation have been, and where we're headed. As the current cycle plays itself out, the course of events, the *Sturm und Drang* (literally 'storm and stress') created will have a major influence on the epic precious metals' uptrend in which we're currently involved. This *zeitgeist* has the potential to extend and exacerbate the levels to which gold, silver and the miners will ascend, prior to their inevitable blow-off.

There are three ways to interpret history. It can be seen as chaotic, linear or cyclical. Strauss and Howe chose the third interpretation. They looked at the Roman concept of the "saeculum" - the theory that history runs in 80 - 100 year cycles. From this concept the authors observed that a human cycle of four generations concludes with a crisis, which leads inevitably to rebirth - and development of an entirely new cycle.

A *turning* is a unit of history that spans roughly a social generation of 20 years or so. The authors conducted a detailed, multiple-century study of the United States, as well as a number of other countries around the world. They discovered the idea of "turnings" as they apply to generational history. As it moves through its life cycle, each generation is different, yet according to the authors, these generations in composite "tend to arrive in a certain pattern, a certain order. Certain types of generations always follow other types. And this in turn is connected to a certain order and rhythm in history itself."

Bernie Quigley describes their work eloquently, writing, "it is a remarkable picture over time, giving history a series of interweaving paths, ascending and returning, like the patterns on the ceiling of the mosque at Cordoba, removing the categorical quality of events which form history and finding instead something more akin to the river of life."

The Boston Globe wrote *If Howe and Strauss are right, they will take their place among the great American prophets.* We believe they are.

The Fourth Turning text (Courtesy Neil Howe)

The groundwork for this book was laid with the publication in 1991, of *Generations,* wherein they discussed America's evolution through the lens of generational biographies. Each ages and moves into its next life phase, maintaining an attachment with the one which preceded it. The terminology the authors use to delineate each interval or "turning" is as follows:

The First Turning is a *High*
– Old values are replaced by a new civic order, with strong social institutions.

The Second Turning is an *Awakening*
– An idealistic and spiritual awakening, with the civic order under attack.

The Third Turning is an *Unraveling*
– Institutions weaken as trust is lost, and individualism strengthens.

The Fourth Turning is a *Crisis*
– One or more unexpected, seminal events shock the nation into action.

Following a crisis (or crises) and a cataclysmic drift wherein society's strongest institutions collapse or narrowly avoid doing so, a new redefined civic order replaces the old one. From our current vantage, we seem to be about half way through this Fourth Turning.

As the third phase progresses, unresolved issues continue to percolate, rising to the surface, increasing the tempo of concern. Some type of catalyst initiates the fourth phase. Increasingly there is a feeling that society is losing control, that the country's moorings are tearing loose, that something different needs to be done. A major war may or may not become a part of the equation. Eventually the population lurches in a particular direction, with the zeitgeist driven by a feeling that an entirely new way of problem-solving is necessary - and urgent.

Strauss and Howe state that America's most recently completed Fourth Turning began with the stock market crash of 1929, and climaxed with World War II (resolving itself at war's end in late 1945). Not everyone is in agreement as to what the catalyst which initiated the current Fourth Turning was, but considering an event of a systemic nature, the 2008 global financial near-meltdown, and its attendant issues - unresolved to the present day - rank it in first place, with 9/11 probably running a close second.

In 1995 Strauss and Howe wrote,

> "Around 2005, a sudden spark will catalyze a Crisis Mood – hardship will beset the land...Around 2025, America will pass through a great gate in history, equivalent to the American Revolution, Civil War, Depression, WW II. The risk of catastrophe will be great...The Fourth Turning could literally destroy us as a nation and people, leaving us cursed in the histories of those who endure and remember.
>
> "Alternatively, it could ennoble our lives, elevate us as a community, and inspire acts of consummate heroism... The rhythms of history do not reveal the outcome of the coming Crisis; **all they suggest is the timing and dimension.**"

Millennials - the "Hero" archetype generation

The members of the new generation who will take the reins, and for better or worse, attempt to lead the country out of its systemically-failed condition, are the Millennials (born 1982 - 2004). They will take this role upon themselves, not because they want to, or are operating out of idealism, but rather because it is imperative that they do so.

Even before the authors had written *The Fourth Turning*, they had in their previously published, *Generations*, coined the term "Millennials". Their studies had shown them the nonlinear path that future generations travel, especially so in regards to this particular one.

In a Forbes interview, Neil Howe remarked, "When we saw Millennials as kids being raised so differently, we could already make an easy prediction. We had seen this dark to bright contrast in child upbringing before many times in American history, so we already foresaw that by the time you got to 2000 you would see huge changes in people in their late teens and early 20s."

Clif Droke, in "The Millennial Moment and the Global Crisis" writes in part:

> "The theory of human endeavor rhythms states that a rising generation, full of energy and ambition, will by its combined productive powers create technologies and innovations which are unique to them. This outpouring of creative energy produces the corresponding need for capital. This is where the stock market comes in and it explains why each generational long-wave is accompanied by a super bull market in equities.
>
> "Each American generation of the last 120 years has had its own Super Cycle bull market... The Millennial generation is the next in line to be served. Born between [1982 and 2004] the Millennials recently surpassed the Baby Boomers as America's largest generation by numbers. They are by far the most educated and tech-savvy generation in America's history and they have the potential to create an economic super boom rivaling the long-wave boom created by the Baby Boomers...
>
> "The Millennial generation is unique among American generations of the last century in that it has had to delay the gratification of its consumerist tendencies just as they've entered their prime years. This will inevitably lead to an explosive release of pent-up energy when the time arrives for them to be served. When the Millennial Moment finally arrives, in other words, it will be huge."

Droke's thesis does not appear to be overstated. According to Census Bureau data, Millennials have become the most populous adult segment in U.S. history, at over 83 million. And they are expected to control between $19 - 24 trillion on a global scale. Baby Boomers, on the other hand, number around 75 million.

John Mauldin echoes Droke's contention, speaking about Millennials - one of the primary demographics our book addresses. He says,

"You really do want to get to the other side of what I see as the coming crisis, too, because on the other side will be one hellacious bull market. Technology is going to take us to places we have never dreamed of. Three billion people are coming into the emerging-market middle classes, even if later rather than sooner. It is going to be a phenomenal world. You have just got to figure out how to get your assets from here to there."

About the "Hero" generation, Frank Holmes at usfunds.com concludes that, "There's no getting around it: Millennials are our future leaders, innovators, consumers and investors. By 2020—a mere four years from now—they will make up an estimated 50 percent of the global workforce."

The *Second Chance* Authors' Gift to Millennials - and Boomers

If as writers, we perform our job well, and if our message reaches the widest audience, we may be able to offer by our suggestions, "a financial leg up" for Millennials. As a group, they have thus far not yet been able to reach the financial and professional levels their parents - many of whom are Baby Boomers - had attained by this stage of their lives. Some - we hope many - will seize the opportunities within the risks that the fourth iteration of the current cycle offers them, so that they may emerge as an independent financial force by which a new and more enduring society can be constructed.

Howe's conclusion serves to empower those willing to reflect and act upon its wisdom:

"Those who understand the rhythms of history can also look for ways to anticipate them—and, thereby, make use of them. In business and investment as in government, marketing, HR, strategic planning, education, and many other areas, the people who succeed in a Fourth Turning mood will be those who understand how history creates generations, and generations create history."

The second major group our book seeks to reach - the Baby Boomers, may in part by following some of the strategies we suggest, enhance their own finances enough so that they can become a supportive force. Change-agents in support of Millennial-aged politicians, as they take over the responsibilities of power, and move to renegotiate the stifling burdens of the social contract put in place, originally with good intentions, during the Great Depression. These burdens have been continually expanded by politicians whose overriding motivation was to get re-elected and continue to feed at the public trough, "until death do they part."

Unceasingly adding to the expense for Social Security, Medicare, prescription benefits and other government transfer programs for retirees. Maintaining the fiction of a "Social Security Lockbox" which is virtually empty, because a given year's SS surplus from paid out benefits was placed, not in a "lock box" - but into the federal government's general fund and doled out as pork by politicians. Legislators who no longer served the people, but rather now run a racket, defined as "of the politicians, by the politicians, and for the politicians."

The Broken Promise

Addison Wiggins speaks to how what was once deemed the governing class has now become the ruling class, when he writes,

"The Age of the Broken Promise is upon us...The Power of the government relies on the power of confiscation – the power to confiscate money, liberty, rights, property, dignity, opportunity, hope...or all at once. But the governments of the West are starting to run out of things to confiscate...the most reliable government guarantee of all is the guarantee that a government will attempt to abrogate its responsibilities and default on its promises."

The American Experience

One of the great things about "the American Experience" is that during times of extreme dislocation, the citizenry has been willing to "chip in and share the burden." Post-Civil War Reconstruction, with all its shortcomings got the U.S. back into a long-term healing mode and ever so slowly set the stage for many of the improvements we see today.

We came out of the Great Depression, achieved victory over the Axis Powers in WW II, and avoided a nuclear holocaust through the present day. So far we have not meaningfully dealt with the current systemic issues that will inevitably take us, according to Howe and Strauss - around the first quarter century mark - to our date with destiny.

Your authors understand this state of affairs quite well, having spoken and written about them for a number of years. We have, as the saying goes, "A dog in the fight." We're Boomers ourselves, and each of our 4 children are Millennials. We'd like to be on the "change-agent team" helping to bequeath an optimal set of circumstances so that our children can have, not just as good a life as we had - but better - much better!

The Boomers - a Wave within the Wave

Our book, *Second Chance,* has long been in the thought process stage prior to making it available to you. Originally, a portion of the title was going to be "The Silver Tsunami." Then we found that the phrase had been taken. It was used in reference to the graying of the Baby Boom generation, now more commonly referred to as "Boomers" - Americans born between 1946 and 1964. We contacted its originator, Dr. Mary Finn Maples, at the University of Nevada, Reno, and received permission to use it, but over time, we came up with another title. However, the topic to which Dr. Maples' term referred is, if anything, even more relevant today than it was when she was writing about it in 2003.

The Boomer generation continues to leave its imprint on the American consciousness and has helped to fashion its history to an extent as outsized as the magnitude of their numbers. They've been trendsetters and newsmakers at every turn. They are becoming eligible for Social Security at the rate of 10,000 per day for the next decade. Soon they will be confronted by the financial impact their numbers will have on a retirement and medical system that the country at large may not be willing - or able to afford. It is beyond the scope of our book to fully detail the pros and cons of this issue, but must be mentioned, because it's definitely not going to just take care of itself.

So far, creative accounting and pie in the sky promises have served to keep the so-called "safety net" on its feet, but we suspect the day will come - during the final years of The Fourth Turning, when this social contract with the Boomers and the generation which follows - the Millennials will have to be severely modified, if not abrogated.

Government bears more than its share of the blame for the fix we have found ourselves in, but there's plenty of responsibility to go around. Is it harsh to say that "Maybe we should not have been so trusting when the politicians spoke to us of a Social Security "lock box." Not to mention when they doled out increasing benefits like prescription drug plans, even as the number of current workers supporting retirees dropped [from over 40:1 to less than one-tenth that number] The statistics below will frighten almost anyone who understands the implications:

- Of current retirees, 60% have less than $25,000 in total savings and investments.
- Of those, 36% have less than $10,000, exclusive of pensions and Social Security.
- Many Boomers are trying to live on Mortgage Equity Withdrawals (MEWs -not eating their felines, as in Venezuela...yet)

Herein lies a message for Baby Boomers. We address especially those who have accumulated a certain amount of investible funds beyond what is needed for everyday expenses, and who have savings left over to provide a financial cushion. They may want to go through the steps of the Boyd Cycle - Observe, Orient, Decide, Act - which we discussed in an earlier chapter.

Because so few are prepared financially, many retirees will try and make up for their lack of saving, and literally pour into the precious metals using any means possible. Some may in fact succeed and we hope that is the case. However, most will be buying during the concluding part of the final phase, thinking they have "made up for lost time", only to discover they stayed too long in what seemed at the time to be "a sure thing."

Whether you're a Millennial or a Boomer, pay attention to detail, invest conservatively, avoid becoming too greedy, and then with a bit of luck, you just might be able to exceed your expectations by a substantial amount!

"It will be a damn close-run thing."

We began this book by telling you that a financial tsunami of unimaginable force is on the way to our shores. It's been building since the 2008 global economic near-collapse. Over the next few years, we'll be buffeted by follow on shock-waves. The sociopolitical discord will be wrenching, at times threatening to rip the nation asunder. A major war - if so, hopefully an external one - is quite possible. Ultimately the Old Guard, and the dis-functional ways of doing things will be cast into history's dustbin. A new paradigm, with new rules to succeed can then be developed.

The readers of this book, subscribers to *The Morgan Report*, and our audiences at conferences around the country, know from observation and personal experience that there exists, at all levels of governance, deeply-embedded, systemic deficiencies and a Protected Class. This group, along with an enlarged "entitlement cohort", will not give up the smallest part of their prerogatives easily. The deep state denizens aren't going to voluntarily stop their march to an even greater acquisition of power and wealth - at the ongoing expense of the liberty and welfare of the overwhelming majority. It will not be easy to combat this, nor will success be foreordained.

As Strauss and Howe themselves write, the outcome cannot be predicted. However, what can be stated categorically, is that we as a nation *will* pass through that Great Gate. In the process, with a lot of work and no small amount of luck, we will hopefully come out the other side in one piece.

As The Fourth Turning plays itself out, we will see the Millennials reacting to the mid-life generation that had previously been in charge, step to the fore, taking over the reins of power and transformation. As stated, we have a vested interest and feel personally responsible to do our share in helping them onto a successful path with their endeavors.

A British Admiral, interviewed years ago about the Allies eventual victory in WW II, had this to say. "Yes we did win... But it was a damn close-run thing!" Something to keep in mind...

Getting to the other side

We are guardedly optimistic that the best of what we as a nation are about will ultimately prevail. Winston Churchill, one of the most trenchant observers of the American Condition since Alexis de Tocqueville, once remarked that "Americans always do the right thing... after they've tried everything else!" From our current perspective it does not appear we've finished trying things that don't work, but hopefully we're getting close!

Robotics, Artificial Intelligence, and 3-D printing will show us a much different future. Eventually there will likely be mining in space and a continuing revolution in nanotechnology. Either or both of these activities may one day put the skids for a very long time to come, on supply issues which have led to price moon shots for certain metals and minerals.

You can be pardoned for wondering if it will ever be possible to roll back the invasive, self-perpetuating, insatiable power of the deep state -of the desire by this modern version of the Mandarin class to do exactly as they want - and force the rest of us to do the same.

But down the line, what Doug Casey refers to as the ongoing Ascent of Man - and Woman, could auger well for us as a nation. It will take enough capable people of good will coming together, guided by politicians who ascend to high office, more in the mold of an Aurelius or a Cincinnatus than a Caligula. That is if they can be kept honest and "sequestered" by a renewed attention to the Constitution, as well as by the power of the Internet to see and report on all things they might do which are untoward. Establishing and maintaining more equitable and effective ways to coordinate better with less governance, re-establishing a system "of the people, by the people, and for the people" would be an excellent prelude to a contemporary "High" - the first turn of the new secular cycle to which Strauss and Howe refer.

These very real possibilities, combined with advances in medicine, nutrition, science, and a willingness to work together to save the planet, have the potential, with the ascendance to positions of responsibility of the Millennials, supported by the Boomers as they step off the stage - to usher in a new Golden Age. We just need to survive in order to get there!

After the Deluge:

After the late Richard Russell, Doug Casey, arguably the doyen of resource sector analysts and speakers, world travelers, and observers of the human condition, had this (as part of a much larger treatise on the subject) to say about the prospects for humanity going forward:

> "I agree that bad things can happen. It's not just a question of misfeasance, some unforeseen accident happening. But actual malfeasance isn't out of the question. Technology is advancing exponentially, but human ethics don't seem to be advancing at all. In fact, maybe the general moral tone of humanity is actually degrading. If that's true, then you can argue it's a bad idea for large-brained chimpanzees to have the magic technologies we've been discussing.
>
> "So, of course, some people will say: 'We have to slow down this mad rush to the future! We have to at least regulate these scary things!' Sound reasonable? Actually, no; the concept is incredibly stupid..."

Doug notes that it tends to be the "leaders"- almost never the best and the brightest - who are the initial recipients of the newest inventions. He goes on to say that,

> "They're actually the worst and most dangerous of mankind, and they're always fearful of progress. Because although the leaders always get new technologies first (e.g., horses, gunpowder, computers), the cat always gets out of the bag, and these things act to further liberate the average man after a while...
>
> "Notwithstanding various drags on our progress, mankind has been expanding its powers exponentially since about the time it learned to make fire. But the nature of the math is that the real growth doesn't come until the end, at which point it seems instantaneous. We can see what's happening intellectually, but very few can picture it in reality.
>
> "It's been said that any sufficiently advanced technology is indistinguishable from magic. But there's

a big problem for you and me as individuals. At the moment, we all have very finite lifetimes... That's why there's absolutely nothing to be lost by going for the brass ring.

"Let's consider mundane life the way it's always been and still is. Unless things change very quickly for the better, you're going to be dead sometime in between tomorrow morning and, if you're both young and lucky, 50 years from now. Considering the (current) absolute and total certainty of death, taking any risk to avoid it, even with long-shot odds, doesn't just make excellent sense. It's imperative..."

By happenstance, Doug Casey's concluding words travel like an arrow to those who desire to better themselves financially - doing well - so that they can do good for their families, deserving others with whom they come into contact, and for themselves too. In the process, rather than becoming a drag on society, they will have become an asset to it.

His words should resonate with people of all ages - the Boomers, Millennials or any other generation who wishes to be part of the positive and enduring change which Doug Casey - and the Authors of *Second Chance* - desire to see come to fruition. This is all highly possible as we leave the far edge of the financial hurricane - the Greater Depression Doug has long predicted, and pass through the Great Gate of Strauss and Howe's *Fourth Turning*. He writes,

"You might ask why investment results even matter if we move into an economy of total abundance. Almost everyone will benefit from these changes, at least indirectly and eventually, if they live long enough. But you want to benefit as directly and immediately as possible. Having capital will put you first in line. Having capital allows you to be an early adopter, and that could be critical. Furthermore, earning capital makes you deserving of that place."

"Strong, secure passwords" - from a Seventh Grader.

As our manuscript was going to the publishers, we ran across a fascinating example of what creativity and the human spirit can accomplish if given some leeway on the put-together side, and allowed a "test-drive" in the marketplace, where consumer needs and entrepreneurial innovation intersect. At http://www.dicewarepasswords.com/ its innovative genius is a seventh grader from New York City. She creates "strong, secure passwords" which she sells for $2 each, derived from using a previously-existing methodology called "Diceware". As described in the New York Daily news, she rolls the dice several times to generate random numbers, which are matched to an index of English words - generating word strings of random phrases. Reportedly, a six word phrase would take a super computer over three thousand years to crack.

The student, Mira Modi now runs a little business, mostly on the weekends, because she doesn't have much time during the week, given she has a lot of schoolwork. She handwrites the codes on paper for her customers, and sends it to them by... snail mail!

As we conclude this chapter - and our book - we want to mention an individual who has done, and continues to perform, much good in the world. His name is Foster Gamble. He and his wife, Kimberly, created the movie *Thrive*. Interviewed by David Morgan on his subscriber-accessed Master Minds, he recounted some of his philosophy - an outlook which we believe is especially relevant to both Millennials and Boomers as we move forward.

Born into a life of great privilege, yet striking out on his own to study for the betterment of humankind, Gamble reached the conclusion that "the fundamental shape, the fundamental wholeness at the human level - is the individual human being, not the group. <u>A real group, a true community, is made up of sovereign individuals coming together.</u>

> "Out of that, price gets determined and resources get distributed accordingly... For me, it's about recognizing that the protection of individual rights is also the protection of economic rights. The more this is done, the more it leads to prosperity, security, happiness and true community."

Gamble envisions, through his "Action 'U'" and other approaches, systemic breakthroughs which have the potential to transform ideas into functional reality. Where the philosophy of liberty that actually includes everyone and a free market economy that honors everyone's transactions..."And breaking through into a completely new paradigm where there are laws but they're only protective laws. There are rules but no rulers, where no one has rights that everyone else does not have."

David Morgan's interview with Foster Gamble was multifaceted. Our feeling is that it will be people like Foster and Kimberly who will find themselves at the vanguard of the change waves which will move our society forward. In positive, productive and enduring ways that will benefit the largest possible number of people. A complimentary copy of the interview can be obtained by writing to support@themorganreport.com

We intentionally included this chapter about the Millennials and the Boomers, to let them know that in the midst of the coming turmoil, there is much they can do to become and remain masters of their fate. Visualize an analogy where all the chairs in a room are unoccupied. In those circumstances, would it not be easier to choose a spot you might like, than if someone was firmly seated in each one?

Canadian Gold Maple Leafs

You see, *Second Chance: How to Make and Keep Big Money from the Coming Gold and Silver Shock-Wave*, is about a lot more than just how to become wealthy, live in luxury and surround yourself with toys and sycophants. Like Doug has also famously said, "There are no luggage racks on a hearse!" So, help yourself by investing wisely, leaving the party early with the majority of your winnings, and seeing how much good you can do from having done well. Live and Love Fully and Wisely.

Doug Casey did not invent the following perspective, nor did we. It's been around for a very long time, and we can all benefit from being reminded about it. In the 700's AD, during what has been called the "Golden Age of China" the great poet Li Bo said profoundly and simply,

"All pomp and circumstance, all wealth and power, are like clouds passing by."

RESOURCES

Website: www.TheMorganReport.com
Twitter @silverguru22
YouTube silverguru
Previous Books-Get the Skinny on Silver Investing, Silver Manifesto

Research/ Education
Riches in Resources Report – Free at http://www.themorganreport.com/
The Mises Institute: https://mises.org/
The Four Horsemen film: fourhorsemenfilm.com
Hidden Secrets of Money: hiddensecretsofmoney.com
Thrive (Foster Gamble) http://www.thrivemovement.com/home
Koos Jansen: https://www.bullionstar.com
Americas Great Awakening: http://americasgreatawakening.com/
David Stockman http://davidstockmanscontracorner.com/
John Williams: http://www.shadowstats.com/
Kitco.com http://www.kitco.com/
Mining.com http://www.mining.com/
Steve Rocco: https://srsroccoreport.com/

Silver Studies
The Silver Institute: http://www.silverinstitute.org/site/
CPM Group: cpmgroup.com
Gold Anti-Trust Action Committee: http://www.gata.org/
Society for Mining, Metallurgy and Exploration: http://www.smenet.org/
USA Watchdog http://usawatchdog.com/
GoldSilver.com https://goldsilver.com/

Recommended Reading:

Economics:
Human Action – Mises
Money, Credit & Economic Cycles – de Soto
What has the Government Done to Our Money? – Rothbard
The Road to Serfdom – Hayek
The Mystery of Banking – Rothbard
The Case Against the Fed – Rothbard
End the Fed – Rothbard
Deflation and Liberty – Hulsmann
Law, Legislation and Liberty
The Law – Bastiat
Capitalism: The Unknown Ideal
The Black Swan: The Impact of the Highly Improbable
Individualism and Economic Order

Investing:
Financial Statement Analysis: Ben Graham
Security Analysis: Graham
Financial Statement Analysis and Security Valuation: Penman
The Dark-side of Valuation: Damodoran
The Intelligent Investor: Graham
The Most Important Thing
Reminiscences of a Stock Operator: Lefevre
Technical Analysis of Stock Trends: Robert D. Edwards and John Magee
The New Case for Gold: Jim Rickards
Nobody Knows Anything: Learn to Ignore the Experts, The Gurus and Other Fools:Moriarty
Common Stocks and Uncommon Profits
The Dao of Capital
Bull: A History of the Boom and Bust 1982-2004
Evaluating Mineral Projects: Applications and Misconceptions: Torries

Websites of Interest

Commodity Online	http://www.commodityonline.com/
Hard Assets Investor	http://www.etf.com/
Safe Haven	http://safehaven.com/
Zero Hedge	http://www.zerohedge.com/
Jesse's Cafe Americain	http://jessescrossroadscafe.blogspot.com/
Max Keiser Fin War Rept.	http://www.maxkeiser.com/
The Gold and Oil Guy	http://www.thegoldandoilguy.com/
David Stockman	http://davidstockmanscontracorner.com/
Gold Miner Pulse	http://goldminerpulse.com/
Junior Mining Network	https://www.juniorminingnetwork.com/
Mining Stock Report	http://miningstockreport.com/
Mining.com	http://www.mining.com/
The Gold Report	http://thegoldreport.com/
Gold-Eagle.com	http://www.gold-eagle.com/
321Gold	http://321gold.com/
Gold Stock Bull	http://goldstockbull.com/
Gold Money	https://www.goldmoney.com/
Run to Gold	http://www.runtogold.com/
Gold Editor	http://www4.goldeditor.com/
Dont-tread-on.me	http://dont-tread-on.me/
TF Metals Report	http://www.tfmetalsreport.com/
Mineweb	http://www.mineweb.com/
Stockcharts.com	http://stockcharts.com/
Barchart.com	http://www.barchart.com/

It is impossible to list all of the websites we visit. In this age of "over-information" some will no doubt change, or perhaps disappear in the future. These will give you a good start.